THINKING AND LEARNING WITH ICT

Primary teachers need to incorporate the use of computers in their daily lesson plans, but how can this be done most effectively to promote learning skills in the classroom? In this fascinating book, the authors outline a strategy for enhancing the effectiveness of computers for teaching and learning with an emphasis on:

- Raising pupil achievement in the core subject areas.
- Developing collaborative learning in small groups.
- Using group discussion as a way of improving general communication, as well as thinking and reasoning skills.

The approach is to use computers as a support for collaborative learning in small groups and the book presents ways to prepare pupils for talking, learning and thinking together around computers. Excerpts from pupils' discussions illustrate the main issues and guidance on lesson planning and developing, and choosing appropriate software is also provided.

Thinking and Learning with ICT will be a valuable resource for primary teachers and student teachers.

Rupert Wegerif is Senior Research Fellow at The Open University. **Lyn Dawes** was previously Education Software Officer at BECTA and is now Senior Lecturer in Primary Education at De Montfort University.

THINKING AND LEARNING WITH ICT

Raising achievement in primary classrooms

Rupert Wegerif and Lyn Dawes

LONDON AND NEW YORK

First published 2004
by RoutledgeFalmer
11 New Fetter Lane, London EC4P 4EE

Simultaneously published in the USA and Canada
by RoutledgeFalmer
29 West 35th Street, New York, NY 10001

RoutledgeFalmer is an imprint of the Taylor & Francis Group

Typeset in Sabon by
Newgen Imaging Systems (P) Ltd, Chennai, India
Printed and bound in Great Britain by
TJ International Ltd, Padstow, Cornwall

British Library Cataloguing in Publication Data
A catalogue record for this book is available from the British Library

Library of Congress Cataloging in Publication Data
Wegerif, Rupert, 1959–
Thinking and learning with ICT : raising achievement in primary classrooms / Rupert Wegerif and Lyn Dawes.
p. cm.
Includes bibliographical references and index.
1. Education – Great Britain – Data processing. 2. Computers and children. 3. Thought and thinking. 4. Education, Elementary – Computer-assisted instruction – Great Britain. I. Dawes, Lyn. II. Title.

LB1028.43.W43 2004
371.33′4–dc22 2003027019

ISBN 0–415–30475–X (hardback: alk. paper)
ISBN 0–415–30476–8 (paperback: alk. paper)

TO JULIETA AND JEAN

CONTENTS

ILLUSTRATIONS

Figures

Table

SEQUENCES OF DIALOGUE

ACKNOWLEDGEMENTS

We are grateful for the support of all the schools, teachers and children in the Milton Keynes area who have helped with the research that we describe. We acknowledge with gratitude the funding that we have received to conduct this research from the Nuffield Foundation, the Esmée Fairbairn Foundation, the Economic and Social Research Council, and Milton Keynes Council who have all funded research projects and from Nesta Futurelab who generously supported the preparation of a literature review.

This book draws heavily on ideas and research findings that were produced through the work of a team of people, the Thinking Together team including Neil Mercer, Karen Littleton, Claire Sams, Steve Higgins, Denise Rowe, Manuel Fernandez and Jan English.

We would also like to thank all our colleagues and friends who provided us with material for the book and with comments on draft texts. These include Karen Littleton, Avril Loveless, Jenny Houssart, Denise Rowe, Neil Mercer, Manuel Fernandez, Bridget Cooper, Steve Higgins and Steve Williams.

We would also like to thank Granada Media for providing free software for our research projects and copyright permission for Figure 6.1 as well as Brenda and Stuart Naylor of Concept Cartoons for copyright permission to use Figure 6.4. John Raven deserves special thanks for the trouble he took to help us with the special Raven's test pictures used in Chapter 3.

A NOTE ON TRANSCRIPTIONS

The names of all the children used in transcriptions of classroom talk have been changed. Transcripts are punctuated to make them as readable as possible. The following conventions, or a sub-set of them, are used throughout:

/	a short pause of less than one second
(2)	a pause of about two seconds
=	where one speaker follows another with no noticeable pause
[	
]	overlapping utterances
(...)	a section of unintelligible speech

INTRODUCTION

Learning with computers in schools is a social activity in which the teacher plays a crucial role. The Thinking Together approach[1] described in this book uses computer-based activities to support collaborative learning in small groups. Children are provided with direct teaching of speaking and listening skills to prepare them for talking, learning and thinking together as they use ICT (Information and Communications Technology). Such preparation for group work with computers, when combined with appropriate ICT tasks and lesson planning, can significantly improve children's achievement throughout the curriculum.

There has been intense interest in finding out if computers really can make a difference to children's learning. It has been difficult to see an overall picture partly because of the continuing evolution of new technology and the variety of ways teachers and learners have found to use computers in classrooms. While some evaluations have demonstrated that the use of ICT can support teaching and learning, others have found that it is hard to attribute learning gains directly to the use of computers. To understand thinking and learning with ICT seems to require not only an examination of individuals or groups at work, but also requires that research looks up from children at computers and investigates their surroundings. In doing so, a general research finding is that the involvement of the teacher in planning, structuring and organising ICT-based activities can make a significant difference to learning outcomes for children. Teachers' professional expertise gives them the foresight to set realistic learning objectives, to identify current understanding, to direct learning experiences and negotiate further steps with the learner. That is, teachers can organise and manage the context within which ICT-based activities take place. But what aspects of the contexts that teachers create really matter in terms of ensuring effective computer use?

This is important, because much software has been designed assuming that children's interaction with computers requires little, if any, intervention from the teacher. Tutorial software provides information and tests to see whether the learner can reproduce it. Other, less directive software has resources and tools to stimulate individual learning through play. Edutainment-type software offers games with chances to recall or rehearse items of factual information, with all the motivating interactivity that is such a draw for children. All can be of some use; but only when teachers put them to use and this usually means integrating their use into teaching and learning dialogues in the classroom.

The key aspects of classroom contexts which teachers can organise to help ensure the effectiveness of computer-based activities are as follows:

- the fostering of a classroom community in which learning dialogues take place through and at computers;
- the use of software and applications which support learning dialogues with a focus on curriculum learning;
- the creation of activities which necessitate learning dialogues.

The Russian philosopher of language, Mikhail Bakhtin, defined dialogue as that kind of conversation where there is also shared inquiry (Bakhtin, 1986). A questioning and open attitude is essential to learning dialogues. In learning dialogues differences of views and perspectives are seen as a positive resource. In fact, according to Bakhtin, understanding comes about through dialogues when the words of others elicit from us our own answering words. In learning dialogues, views are offered provisionally with reasons to support them, or the promise of reasons, rather than being simply asserted as truth. Challenges are expected and are welcomed. Contribution by all is actively invited and respected. The participants are aware that through speaking and listening they are thinking together, and that this activity is necessary to promote and consolidate each individual's development of ideas (Mercer, 2000).

Such dialogues can take place not just between teachers and learners, but equally profitably, between learners engaged in a joint task. Understanding how and why to discuss ideas when engaged in ICT-based activities allows learners to 'build coherent and expanding chains of enquiry and understanding' (Alexander, 2002). Throughout this book there are examples of this productive type of dialogue. Many of the examples are drawn from the Thinking Together project which has investigated group work at computers for more than a decade. Thinking Together provides children with direct teaching of speaking and listening skills to prepare them for talking, learning and thinking together as they use ICT. Such preparation, when combined with appropriate ICT tasks, lesson planning and teacher intervention, can significantly improve children's achievement throughout the curriculum. This book describes the Thinking Together approach, the associated research studies and their findings, in order to help teachers in their crucial role of employing the powerful tools of ICT to good effect.

The strength of this approach depends on creating a classroom in which trust and mutual purpose is established between learners, and between teachers and learners. The Thinking Together research is based on extending this principle to include researchers. In this way classroom practice, research intervention, analysis and discussion are shared enterprises which proceed through equitable dialogue. Promoting effective ways of thinking and learning with computers is considered analogous to promoting effective inter-relationships between research and practice because learning dialogues are required in both contexts.

The book's emphasis on thinking and learning is coupled with a focus on citizenship. The child's individual development of thinking and discussion skills is linked with their understanding of how to employ such skills to further their own learning and that of others. Children taught to collaborate at, around, through and in relation to computers are learning transferable social skills. This interdependence of personal development and social development can positively influence the child's contribution to their community. In the same way, facilitating the acquisition of literacy through ICT use allows the child to gain from and contribute more readily to the literate practices of the communities in which they participate. Positioning the computer as a support for social learning harnesses its power to motivate, resource and stimulate classroom learning to good effect.

About the structure of this book

The first four chapters outline the Thinking Together approach, providing some background information, an account of how to prepare children for work with computers, an explanation of the significance of Thinking Together and an analysis of the role of computers in teaching thinking skills. Part two, Chapters 5–9, look in more detail at how learning dialogues can be organised and sustained in key areas of the curriculum. The book's focus on the curriculum area of citizenship indicates a key concern with the development of the whole child within a community. A concentration on the quality of dialogue within teaching and learning is of benefit for children and for society in the broadest possible terms.

The content of each chapter is described here briefly.

1 *Using computers in classrooms*
Video evidence of children's interaction with one another at the computer enabled teachers to evaluate the quality of group work. They were often disappointed with what they found. Preparing children to work together at computers proved to be an effective way of improving the quality of the learning that resulted.
2 *Teaching children how to talk together*
The Talk Lessons are described in detail. Through these lessons classes establish and use shared ground rules for collaboration such as listening

with respect, responding to challenges with reasons, encouraging partners to give their views and trying to reach agreement. We present research evidence indicating that Talk Lessons can transform the quality of group work around computers.

3 *Thinking Together*
Teaching children how to talk together more effectively is a way of helping them to think more effectively. Examples of small groups solving problems together show the importance of social relationships in the process of learning. This chapter provides the basis for discussion of how computers can be used effectively in group work. It establishes the value of integration of ICT activities based on thinking skills into the curriculum.

4 *Thinking skills and computers*
A review of the research evidence for the various claims that have been made about the relationship between ICT and teaching thinking skills is provided. This suggests that there is little evidence that children learn or assimilate thinking skills simply by using computers. However, there does appear to be good evidence that some ICT-based activities can help teach thinking skills when used as a resource to support learning dialogues. An important factor is the role of the teacher in making the thinking aims of activities explicit, modelling good thinking strategies and designing learning activities so that skills learnt in one context are applied in new contexts.

5 *ICT and citizenship: joining the dialogue*
Talking effectively with others implies the application of a number of values: respect, empathy, a sense of fairness, tolerance for differences and, above all, a rejection of coercive force in favour of persuasion. A focus on dialogue, discussion and reasoning as the medium of teaching and learning can therefore communicate the core values promoted by the citizenship curriculum. Talk can be stimulated by software which is designed to engage young children in moral reasoning about ethical dilemmas. Transcript evidence reveals how software can help children seriously engage in debates about issues that matter to them. Similar principles can be applied to the use of web sites, bulletin boards, email links and conferences to involve children in dialogues about citizenship issues with others beyond their classroom.

6 *Science, talk and ICT*
Children's learning in science requires that they learn how to discuss science concepts and processes, using scientific vocabulary to do so. Children must articulate their initial conceptions of the way the world works so that these can be developed or challenged. One of the most important ideas taught in science is that theories are subject to question and to a process of systematic shared enquiry. Children require guided opportunities to talk in order to understand and apply this idea. The

combination of talk lessons and the appropriate software can prompt questioning, provide support for structuring scientific enquiry and offer resources for experiment and exploration that allow children to develop their own ideas in a way that converges with accepted scientific concepts.

7 *Maths, talk and ICT*
Computer software can bring mathematical rules to life. Through manipulating virtual worlds children are helped to understand the 'artificial reality' of maths. Their talk with the teacher and with one another is crucial to the development of understanding. ICT-based mathematical activities can become a source of general problem-solving strategies that can be applied across the curriculum.

8 *Literacy and ICT*
A combination of computer-based activities and collaborative learning can support the development of literacy. Computers have a special role to play in bridging the transition from oracy to literacy. The relationship between conventional literacy and various forms of digital literacy is examined, as is the close relationship that exists between oracy, literacy and thinking skills. The combination of a Thinking Together approach with a focus on the communication aspect of ICT is particularly important for enabling children to engage in collective thinking.

9 *Learning through dialogue in the ICT curriculum*
While the rest of the book looks at ICT across the curriculum, this chapter focuses on ICT as a subject area. Many aspects of ICT as a subject are naturally suited to collaborative learning. This chapter highlights a collaborative approach to specific applications of technology such as conferencing, email exchanges, use of the Internet and robotics.

10 *Conclusion: raising achievement*
The concluding chapter discussed the role of computers in classrooms and the crucial role of the teacher. This summary establishes how implementation of the Thinking Together approach can help to raise children's achievement across the curriculum.

This book is supported by a web site: http://www.dialoguebox.org. This web site provides some of the software mentioned in the classroom activities described in the book. It also provides further classroom resources and information about the Thinking Together approach.

Part I

TALKING AND THINKING TOGETHER WITH COMPUTERS

1

USING COMPUTERS IN CLASSROOMS

When teachers see video recordings of children's interaction with one another in group work at the computer they are often disappointed with what they find. We describe how preparing children to work together at computers is an effective way of improving the quality of the learning that results from group work at the computer.

When researchers from the Open University visited Zoe Andrew's classroom in the early 1990s they found the air humming with the noise of purposeful activity. Zoe's class of 8-year-old children were working in small groups around different tables. Each group was preparing some text and pictures about an aspect of Viking life. The walls of the spacious modern classroom were covered in colourful displays. At the back of the room, in a corner next to a sink, there was one computer on a trolley with three children sitting around it on stools. They seemed very engaged in what they were doing, staring at the screen, sometimes talking and pointing but without really looking at each other. The software that they were using, Viking England,[1] was a kind of adventure game that allowed them to role-play as a group of Vikings raiding the coast of England to get treasure from the monasteries. They apparently found this very motivating.

Zoe, a young and enthusiastic teacher who was committed to the use of ICT, admitted that she found it hard trying to integrate the use of just one computer with the rest of her teaching. However, she was impressed with the children's enjoyment of their work at the computer and the way in which it managed to hold their attention. She tried to give each of the children in her class as much time on the computer as possible. This was certainly one of her reasons for asking the children to work together around the computer in small groups, but it was not her only reason. She explained that she believed in the value of collaborative learning. She wanted to give the children an opportunity to talk together at the computer because she felt that this was good for the development of their communication skills. In this, Zoe reflected views shared by many primary teachers (Crook, 1994).

Zoe agreed that researchers could video-record groups of children working together around the computer at a range of different types of software. She became part of the government-funded Spoken Language and New Technology (SLANT) project which collected video recordings of primary school children working in pairs or small groups at different kinds of software in a range of schools. Having a video camera and a researcher in the classroom created a bit of a stir at first but the children quickly became used to it. The video recordings were transcribed so that the language used by the children could be examined in detail.

The SLANT team worked closely with all the teachers involved in the project, such as Zoe, in order to try to understand what was really going on when children worked together around computers (Wegerif and Scrimshaw, 1997). Part of this process involved university researchers together with classroom teachers watching the video recordings of children talking in classrooms. There were always so many other things to do in the classroom that Zoe had little opportunity to attend to conversations of groups working at the computer. Usually she left them alone, happy to see them apparently constructively engaged. When she did join them it was often difficult to find out what learning had taken place. The videos were a good chance to look more closely at the children's independent activity while she was working with others in the class. What she saw dismayed her.

Zoe's reaction was common to the teachers in the project. The video recordings enabled teachers to analyse how the children worked together and on the whole, they did not like what they saw.

What was going wrong?

Here is a list of some of the ways that the SLANT team found that children were working together around computers when the teacher was not present.

- One person appointed themselves leader, sitting centrally to the keyboard, and reading from the screen. They called out and entered instantaneous responses to questions. Other members of the group would agree, or start a futile 'Yes it is/No it isn't' exchange.
- Children with home computers would become impatient with others who had no keyboard skills, and would dominate both the keyboard and the decision-taking. Or, a quiet but literate child would work as 'secretary' to a 'dictator'.
- Less confident children would watch, agree, or withdraw, contributing little. If things subsequently seemed to go wrong, they were castigated by other members of the group for 'not helping'.
- Friends at work together agreed with one another readily with no challenge or reflection. Other children always disagreed with whatever was suggested without offering alternatives.

- The content of the talk was to do with a re-establishment of the children's social orientation to one another.
- The most heated discussions were to do with who was seated where, who pressed the next key, and so on. Children spent a lot of time talking about how to make the task of actually operating the computer 'fair' – an impossibility, but of great importance to them.
- Talk became general and relaxed if the computer was sited out of the teacher's natural range. This was possibly because children realised that concentrating on the work would mean that their long-awaited turn at the computer would be over sooner and so they chatted about other things.
- Children competed within the group, using the computer program as a game of some sort. Useless disputes ensued without a constructive outcome. Sometimes children became distressed by the criticism they received and left the group 'playing on the computer' to 'go back to work'.

Improving the quality of talk

Looking at the videos it became clear that one of the problems, perhaps the main problem, was that the children were trying to work together but did not really know how to do this effectively. The Thinking Together team decided that some 'pre-computer' activities could perhaps prepare children better and help them gain more from their work together. This was the beginning of the creation of the 'Talk Lessons' – a set of lessons for teaching children the crucial importance of their talk together. Further information about the Talk Lessons is contained in Chapter 2.

The Talk Lessons focused on teaching children how to ask each other questions and then respond with reasons. For example, one lesson concentrated on ensuring that children knew how to ask each other 'What do you think? And why do you think that?' and how to respond to such a challenge by saying 'I think... because...'. No doubt the children already knew how to ask 'why?' and use 'because' in other contexts. The problem was not necessarily that they did not know how to question and to reason but that they were not applying this knowledge when working in a group in the classroom. As well as teaching ways of using spoken language the lessons set up clear expectations in the children's minds as to how they should talk with each other whenever they were asked to work together around a computer.

Children working together after undertaking the initial Talk Lessons responded very differently to one another and the computer. Invited to witness this, the Thinking Together team video-recorded a group from the class working with software called 'Viking England'. This programme allows children to imagine that they are Vikings planning and then executing a raid on the coast of England. The difference in the quality of their talk from all the other recordings was immediately apparent.

The two boys and a girl in the group video recorded were not chosen for their good behaviour. One of the boys, who we will call Randall, was constantly unsettled in class and had recently been provided with a Statement of Special Educational Need for his emotional and behavioural difficulties.

In the past there had often been tension between the members of this group. But what we found when we looked at the video was that the group were not simply interacting more productively with the computer programme; they were also more attentive to each other.

Sequence 1.1, 'Planning a raid', gives an idea of what we mean by claiming that the children's talk was of good quality. Diana, Randall and Andy are sitting around a computer screen which is displaying a map of the East coast of England. Four sites are marked with symbols indicating key features such as monasteries, settlements and rocky coastline. Before we join them the computer has asked the group, in their role as Vikings, to select one of these four monasteries to 'raid'.

Sequence 1.1 Planning a raid

DIANA: Let's discuss it.
RANDALL: Which one shall we go for?
DIANA: We've got to discuss it.
RANDALL: Three (...) are unopposed (...) left in the area. So if we took 1 we have got more of a chance of getting more money because...
DIANA: And if we take number 2 there's that monastery over there and...
RANDALL: Yeh but yeh, because the huts will be guarded.
DIANA: Yeh.
RANDALL: And that will probably be guarded.
DIANA: It's surrounded by trees.
RANDALL: Yeh.
ANDY: And there's a rock guarding us there.
RANDALL: Yes there's some rocks there. So I think...I think it should be 1.
ANDY: Because the monastery might be unguarded.
RANDALL: Yeh but what about 2 that...it might be not guarded. Just because there's huts there it doesn't mean it's not guarded does it. What do you think?
DIANA: Yes it doesn't mean it's not. It doesn't mean to say it's not guarded does it? It may well be guarded. I think we should go for number 1 because I'm pretty sure it's not guarded.
ANDY: Yeh.
RANDALL: OK. Yes. Number 1.
(Andy keys in number 1 and Randall presses the return key).
ANDY: (Reads from screen) 'You have chosen to raid area 1'.

Here you can see all the children involved in solving a problem together. They make suggestions, challenge one other, give reasons and finally agree on what the group considers to be the best alternative. One criticism of this talk, from an educational point of view, might be that it is not evident that the children are learning very much about the Vikings. The exciting thing for the SLANT team at this point was not the effect on curriculum learning so much as the quality of the talk. In further chapters, we will explore how this kind of talk can be harnessed to help raise achievement across the curriculum.

When Diana says 'We've got to discuss it' there is perhaps an echo of the teacher's voice. The children have learned that the purpose of working with a group is to discuss their thoughts when faced with a task like this at the computer. They are motivated by the computer 'game' but also by the understanding that discussing issues will help them do better as a group. The prior Talk Lessons are clearly an influence on the way that this group is talking together. The design of the software also plays a part. The particular task that the computer sets them seems to encourage the children to reason together. Looking at the video recording, it is interesting to see that the children physically point to features marked on the screen to emphasise reasons for choosing one site to raid over another. The importance of the combination of whole class teaching and of software design to produce rich educational experiences at the computer is one of the themes that we will return to throughout this book.

The computer in the conversation

The way that children respond to working with computers in educational settings is crucial. This is something that changed visibly as a result of the Talk Lessons. In most of the video recordings there was much more interaction with the computer interface than talk between the children. Often the groups seemed highly motivated and even fascinated by the interactivity of computer programmes. Usually, if the computer offered a prompt of some sort the children responded almost immediately. If they spoke at all before one of them responded they did so while all facing the screen. However, in the Viking England data something very different can be seen to be happening. In this recording, it was possible to see the children sit back from the computer, look at each other, and try to engage one another in discussion.

The Viking England software that the children were using was very simple. It was a little like many early text and graphic adventure games. It prompted the children with text questions such as 'Look at the map and decide which site are you going to raid: A, B, C or D?' Each choice led to a different outcome, a new graphic and a new question from the computer. We can see the computer's initial feedback in the transcript given here: 'You have chosen to raid area 1'.

IRF: a way of talking commonly used in teaching and learning

To understand the role of the computer, the SLANT team found it useful to draw on the work of linguists who had studied and described classroom talk. One way of considering a basic educational exchange between teachers and learners is as Initiation, Response and Follow-up (IRF) (Sinclair and Coulthard, 1975). A straightforward example of an IRF would be as given here:

TEACHER: What kind of ships did the Vikings use? (Initiation)
STUDENT: Longboats. (Response)
TEACHER: Well done. (Follow-up)

The IRF structure can be used to distinguish educational conversations from other kinds. It is easy to see how this kind of structure allows teachers to monitor what students are learning. Of course there is more to IRF exchanges than this simple example shows. Often teachers will build on a student's response or bring in other students to challenge or elaborate what has been said. The 'Follow-up' move is not always a direct evaluation, such as 'well done', but may be a comment or a follow-up question. Had the answer to the first question here, for example, been 'wooden boats' the teacher might have replied, 'Well done; and can anybody tell me the name that we give to the wooden boats that the Vikings used?'

Much has been written about IRFs in books on education. Some researchers have claimed that IRFs are intrinsically detrimental because they limit the students' ability to construct meaning for themselves (Wood, 1988). More recently, a consensus seems to be emerging that the important thing is not the IRF in itself but what teachers do with the IRF format (Wells, 1999). The key difference seems to be between using IRFs to close down thinking or to draw children in to more extended enquiry. But what interests us about IRFs is that this same structure, found first in exchanges between teachers and students, can also be seen happening in exchanges between computers and students.

I*D*RF: a way of learning with computers

The simple exchange around Viking England, described earlier, appears to fit the IRF framework. The computer software initiates with a question: Which site are you going to raid? (I) The children think about it and respond with one of the four choices offered (R). The computer then acknowledges their choice and gives feedback on it through the next challenge that it selects for them (F). Several people have pointed out that what happens around most educational software fits the IRF talk structure, even so-called 'edutainment' and adventure games (Fisher, 1992). However, IRF is not adequate to describe what happened in the exchange captured in

Sequence 1.1. IRF does not reflect the volume and quality of talk between learners which goes on after the computer initiation and before the response – keying in the number 1 – was entered.

In Sequence 1.1, the children are seen to sit back deliberately from the computer screen and *discuss* what they think before deciding on a joint response. This extra discussion inserted into the IRF exchange transforms the whole educational experience. It introduces a pause for reflection and for thought. By talking together the children construct an understanding of what is going on in their own words. In this example, they generate a mutual understanding of why the Vikings might have preferred to raid some sites rather than others. Such discussion between the 'I' of initiation and the 'R' of response introduces a new and important kind of educational exchange which therefore needs a new name. We call it not simply IRF but I*D*RF which stands for: Initiation, *Discussion*, Response, Follow-up.

The educational significance of I*D*RF

In some ways the I*D*RF idea is very simple. Children working together in groups at computers often talk together. But thinking about their talk as a potential I*D*RF exchange helps to clarify how to promote learning experiences. In other words, I*D*RF is not merely a description but also a design template for effective learning.

The 'IRF' part of I*D*RF refers only to the student–computer interaction. If we look at the IRF exchange alone, the computer appears to direct the learning and the student appears to be fairly passive. Much tutorial software promotes interaction of this kind. The computer gives some information and then asks a question about it with a multiple choice answer. On the other hand, the '*D*' part of I*D*RF refers only to the spoken student to student discussion. Here students may come up with ideas and support them with reasons before testing them out on the computer. Discussion of this kind provides an opportunity for the construction of meaning by students. When they sit back from the computer and discuss a question, perhaps arguing amongst themselves about the preferred response, something interesting happens to their relationship with the computer. Whereas in the IRF sequence the computer appears to be in control, in the '*D*' or discussion activity the students appear to be in control.

If we go back to Sequence 1.1 we can see that the children are deciding which place to land on the east coast of England in a way which involves making hypotheses. 'I think we should raid site 1', says Andy, 'Because it is unguarded' continues Randall. This is a reasoned hypothesis about the best place to raid which they can now test out on the computer. The children are actively putting forward ideas and testing them against one another's ideas before submitting them to the computer. Constructing and testing their hypothesis involves them in thinking together, applying prior knowledge and creativity, and considering alternative ideas. It is while engaged in such dialogues that deep learning takes place.

There is strong evidence that the best kind of learning happens when students find things out for themselves. If, like an IRF tutorial programme, tuition is to do with telling students things and then testing them on what they know, they may remember some of it but often the kind of learning involved can be termed 'shallow'. Shallow learning fades quickly and is difficult to apply to other contexts. The kind of learning that can occur through discussion is quite different. During talk together students often have to struggle to articulate a problem and then to express a solution in their own words. This kind of learning is 'deep', meaning that it is retained longer, is better related to other understanding, and is more likely to be useful in a range of contexts in and out of the classroom (Claxton, 1999).

There are good reasons why educationalists have criticised tutorial software that produces IRF interactions (Papert, 1981). The same writers have often praised more open-ended software which is under students' control and which they can use to explore and construct understandings for themselves. However, education is not a matter of free exploration and unguided discovery. The curriculum, for valid reasons, specifies in advance what students are expected to learn through their education. On the other hand, simply telling students what they are supposed to learn and expecting them to understand is ineffective. Education works best when students are actively involved in their own learning – and when the construction of personal understandings by students is guided by teachers.

The Russian educational psychologist Lev Vygotsky, writing in the 1920s, described this double-sided nature of education. He argued that education at its best brings together two processes: that of spontaneous learning whereby children construct their own understandings, and that of directive teaching through which the existing knowledge of a culture is communicated to children. The key to effective education is therefore the role of the teacher in helping children to learn things for themselves. That is, 'scaffolding' (Wood *et al.*, 1976) their construction of personal meaning. Vygotsky coined the rather awkward phrase 'zone of proximal development' for the gap between what children could do alone and what they could do when working together with a teacher. For any student, there will be problems that they can solve easily on their own and problems that are simply too difficult for them to understand. In between these two extremes, there is a range of problems that they can solve with help. This is the 'zone of proximal development'. It is in this zone, the zone just ahead of their current knowledge, that children can be led to learn new things (Vygotsky, 1986).

What is so exciting about computer-supported I*D*RF interaction is that it achieves the combination of directive teaching and active learning into a single activity. Prompts, information and questions can provide directive teaching while learning conversations enable children to construct new understandings and generate their own questions. In the following chapters, we will describe how this simple IDRF idea can support the effective use of ICT across the curriculum.

Back in the classroom

In the late 1990s, Zoe Andrews' school invested in a suite of computers with Internet connectivity. The science co-ordinator bought data-logging equipment and the art teacher brought in a scanner. Zoe used a digital camera with her class. She visited the BETT educational technology show (held every January at Olympia in London) and started campaigning for the school to acquire an interactive white board. She and her colleagues obtained computers to use for their work at home. The use of technology in classrooms became much more of an everyday occurrence. Importantly, 'Information Technology' was renamed 'Information and Communications Technology' (ICT). This emphasised that technology was not just for transmitting data, but could enable people to exchange ideas and work together through (for example) email and conferencing software. Computers were for collaboration. But however sophisticated the technology, Zoe remained convinced that its educational effectiveness depended enormously on teaching her children how to talk about their work.

Our purpose in writing this book is to share with you ten years' experience of working with teachers using the Talk Lessons approach. In this way, we hope that groups of children using ICT in your schools can be helped to achieve more by working effectively together – and to enjoy the surprisingly exciting experience of engaging with one another in constructive discussion.

Summary

The approach to ICT use described in this book began with a team of researchers and teachers investigating how computers were being used in primary classrooms. Computers have been seen by teachers as a good support for pair and small group work. Video recordings of children working together at computers produced evidence that disappointed teachers. The educational quality of dialogue at computers could be very poor. How well did children understand what was expected of them in terms of their individual contributions to group work? Questions or prompts from the computer can stimulate discussions by pupils which led to the achievement of learning goals. Working closely with teachers, the Thinking Together team developed a way to enhance this productive use of ICT. We called this strategy 'IDRF', referring to an Initiation (I) by the computer leading to pupil Discussion (D) *before a Response (R) by the pupils together and Follow-up (F) move by the computer. With appropriate software and direct teaching of talk skills, group work at computers can generate IDRF exchanges that lead to useful learning.*

2

TEACHING CHILDREN HOW TO TALK TOGETHER

Chapter 1 emphasises the importance of teaching children discussion skills before expecting them to work in collaborative groups around the computer. This chapter describes how that can be done.

Literacy and numeracy have always been given high priority in the British educational system. In contrast, speaking and listening have received intermittent and uncertain attention. But the development of literacy is grounded in a knowledge of language gained through talk in a variety of social settings. Similarly achievement across the curriculum depends on the capacity to understand spoken language. For primary school children talk is the principal medium through which they access education – talk with teachers and classmates provides invaluable opportunities to make meaning from information, articulate new ideas, and solve a range of problems and puzzles.

It is surprising, then, that little or no time is devoted to the direct teaching of the special speaking and listening skills which are crucial for learning in so many areas. Perhaps one reason for this omission is that most children arrive at school already having learnt an impressive amount about talk during their early years. They present themselves with a good working vocabulary and an understanding of all sorts of subtleties concerning grammar and syntax. Some are even bilingual. But there is still much to learn. For example, children need to learn how to talk appropriately and effectively in a range of social contexts. This is a difficult and lengthy task. One concern of teachers should be to help children gain an awareness of what sort of talk will help them to make the most of their time in the classroom. Those children who are adept users of particular sorts of 'educational' discourse can be expected to gain most from their interactions with teachers, peers and the learning activities they are offered.

In this chapter we will focus on a particular way to help children learn the discussion skills that will support their group work at the computer.

Shoot-em-up!

The following example may help to clarify our claim that children's talk shapes what they learn together. It is a transcript taken from a video-recording of two 10-year-old boys, Sean and Lester, working together using mathematics software designed by SMILE to support the teaching of co-ordinates (Mercer, 1995). The software provides a grid representing New York City. An elephant is 'lost' in the city and the aim is to locate it by keying in co-ordinates. After each guess, the programme provides information about how near the guess is to the actual position of the elephant. The programme developers intended that children think about co-ordinates and solve the problem by using the feedback they are given.

Sequence 2.1 Find the elephant

LESTER: I know where it is. (Sean takes his turn and fails to find the elephant.)
LESTER: I told you it weren't over there. (He then takes his turn also without success.)
SEAN: Eh, heh heh heh (laughing gleefully).
LESTER: Which one just went on? I don't know. (Says something unintelligible.)
SEAN: 1, 2, 3, 4, 5, 6 (Counting squares on the screen).
LESTER: I know where it is.
SEAN: I got the nearest.

This disputational talk was not at all what the designers intended. Sean and Lester treated the programme as a competitive game. They took turns to make random guesses not really based on the information the computer offered. They laughed or made derisory comments when their partner made an incorrect guess. They were motivated enough to keep trying until by chance a correct guess was made: at which point either could say with satisfaction 'I won!' – while the other might insist that the game 'wasn't fair'.

There is some evidence that children's main experience of using computers with others outside school is through playing competitive video-games (Selwyn, 1998). The kind of talk Sean and Lester engaged in is what could be expected if they were playing, for example, 'Shoot-'em-up' games with a Playstation. However, this exchange did not help them learn about co-ordinates or to develop problem-solving strategies together. Children who have only ever used computers in order to compete with one another are unlikely to decide spontaneously to pause during a game like 'Elephant in New York' and reflect on how they might collaborate or discuss together the best strategy for understanding and solving the problem.

What are we supposed to say?

Sean and Lester were using a type of talk that has been called 'disputational'. They were treating the activity as an opportunity for conversation focused on self-assertion and self-defence. 'I'm right and you're wrong' might sum it up. This sort of talk, perhaps learned through interaction with adults and peers in a range of contexts, creates problems for children when it interferes with their capacity to collaborate with one another in educational settings. A further problem for children working at computers is that they may be overly concerned with what it is they imagine the teacher wants them to do. The video evidence revealed that children asked to work at the computer often assumed that they were required to produce 'the right answer' or a neatly written end product. They did not seem to realise that a primary aim for their work was that they collaborate through talk.

We noticed this effect very strongly when we designed software to challenge the children to think about moral dilemmas. The programme, Kate's Choice, was designed to integrate with the citizenship curriculum and emphasises the importance of discussion and considering the perspective of others in reaching moral decisions. The story involves two young friends, Kate and Robert. Robert has a box of chocolates and Kate asks where he got them. Robert asks her to promise to keep his secret before he tells her that he stole them. Kate then has to decide whether she should tell her parents about this (see Figure 2.1). The groups are asked to consider the issues and then decide whether Kate should keep Robert's secret. Depending

Figure 2.1 Should Kate tell? A computer prompt.

on which choice they make the groups are then faced with other challenges and moral dilemmas. We piloted this software with 8- and 9-year-old children in a school in an area of high social deprivation. These children made it clear that they did not approve of 'telling' or 'grassing' or of breaking promises. Yet faced with the decision about whether Kate should tell her parents Robert's secret, the children without exception immediately decided that she should. It did not even seem to be a moral dilemma for them. Rather surprised by this, we provided more information about the incident to try to present a more taxing dilemma for the children. We added that Robert's reason for stealing the chocolates for his mother was that it was her birthday and he had no money to buy her a present. This made no difference; again, all the children decided without real discussion that Kate should tell the secret. Again we adapted the story to make the decision more demanding: we added that Robert's mother was ill in hospital. Despite this heart-tugging scenario, all the children still decided that Kate should immediately tell her parents about the theft.

The video recordings of the children's talk together provided insight into their thought processes. They tended not to consider the moral issues. Instead they asked questions such as 'What are we supposed to put?' or 'What does she [*the teacher*] want us to say?' Having considered this, groups agreed with one another that 'stealing is wrong' was the 'right' answer, and so decided that Kate would tell her parents Robert's secret.

It was only when we taught these same children how to 'think together' that they began to understand the purpose of their discussion and to work within the learning intention of the activity, that is to discuss issues such as friendship, shoplifting, truth and lies.

What teachers want

It is interesting that these children assumed that their teachers wanted 'right answers' rather than discussion. But one of the main reasons that teachers give for grouping children at computers is to help their development of oracy and communication skills (Crook, 1994). Over the years, we have asked many groups of primary teachers this question:

> 'What sort of talk would you like to hear happening when you listen to groups of children working together at the computer?'

With some variation in wording, teachers almost all said that they hoped their groups would

- actively listen to each other;
- respect the thoughts and ideas of others in the group;

- compromise if there was disagreement;
- give reasons for opinions, to support arguments or ideas;
- give everyone the opportunity to participate;
- respond to what other people say;
- stay on task;
- share and explain ideas;
- be prepared to change their minds, or negotiate to agree what to do.

These aims match what we call 'Thinking Together'. However, such discussion is unusual at computers when children are not aware of these expectations. Additionally, children may not realise the educational importance of their talk with one another. And even if they do wish to discuss issues and ideas, they may not know how to set about organising such an interchange when no adult is present – such as when working in a group work at the computer.

Developing Talk Lessons

Chapter 1 described how, faced with the evidence of the lack of collaboration amongst groups at computers in her class, a series of 'Talk Lessons' was devised. Since then many sets of talk or Thinking Together lessons have been created for different educational contexts. The form and structure of the Talk Lessons embody teachers' conceptions of what constitutes an educationally effective discussion. In addition, the lessons draw on the findings of educational research into effective collaborative learning and thinking. For example, research has shown, perhaps unsurprisingly, that the best problem-solving occurs in groups where the most alternatives are considered and rejected before a conclusion is reached (Kruger, 1993). Other research has shown that groups with the explicit requirement of reaching a consensus view learn more from discussion of science issues than groups without this expectation (Howe *et al.*, 2000). Our colleague Neil Mercer has provided a definition of 'Exploratory Talk' which he describes as an educationally valued way of talking together:

> Exploratory Talk foregrounds reasoning. Its ground rules require that the views of all participants are sought and considered, that proposals are explicitly stated and evaluated, and that explicit agreement precedes decisions and actions. It is aimed at the achievement of consensus. Exploratory Talk, by incorporating both conflict and the open sharing of ideas represents the more visible pursuit of rational consensus through conversations. It is a speech situation in which everyone is free to express their views and in which the most reasonable views gain acceptance.
>
> (adapted from Mercer, 1995)

This description of Exploratory Talk provides a structure with which you can generate teachable 'ground rules' for talk. Application of the ground rules by groups working at computers provides good opportunities for generating educationally effective discussion.

Ground rules for Exploratory Talk are

- everyone in the group is encouraged to speak by other group members;
- all relevant information is shared;
- reasons are expected;
- contributions are considered with respect;
- challenges are accepted;
- the group takes responsibility for decisions;
- alternatives are discussed before a decision is taken;
- the group seeks to reach agreement.

The various Thinking Together lessons take these ground rules of Exploratory Talk as their starting of point. Early lessons focus on raising an awareness of the importance of talk while developing skills such as listening, sharing information and co-operating. Later lessons encourage critical argument for and against different cases. In the lessons, children are given opportunities to practise discussing alternative ideas, giving and asking for reasons and ensuring that all members of the group are invited to contribute.

Some key features of all the Thinking Together lessons are as follows:

- Learning objectives for group talk are made explicit in the introduction.
- Groups reflect on the quality of their talk in plenary sessions.
- The class is directly taught talk skills such as asking questions, challenging one another, reasoning, negotiating ideas.
- Meaningful contexts are provided to allow children to develop and practice talk skills.
- Classes create and agree on a shared set of ground rules for talk.
- The teacher focuses the class on the quality of their talk, provides intervention to support groups during discussion, and models Exploratory Talk in the way in which she or he talks to the class.
- The outcome of the lesson is not usually written work but a developed understanding which any of the group can rationalise.

For the Talk Lessons, classrooms are organised so that children work in mixed ability groups of three. This provides groups with a range of opinions and ideas and ensures that each group has a fluent reader/writer. Occasionally, pairs and larger groups are used when required by a specific task or the context. To encourage a perception that all contributions to the group work are equal, there are no set 'roles' within the groups, other than that of occasional scribe or reader. Evidence shows that the most confident child may adopt a facilitator or moderator role, acting as a 'discourse guide' to remind others of the ground rules.

Table 2.1 provides an overview of the learning objectives and content of a set of Talk Lessons developed for a project at Key Stage 1. The table indicates how the initial Talk Lessons deal with raising awareness of talk as a tool that supports collaborative work. Basically, after lessons with a focus on raising awareness of the importance of how we talk together (the number of these depending on the age of the children, the time available and teacher evaluation of the children's understanding), the class is asked to work with their teacher to create and decide on their own class set of ground rules for Exploratory Talk. They learn that if they can all use these rules at the computer, they have the best chance to work effectively by reaching decisions based on considering evidence, reasons and shared

Table 2.1 The Talk Lesson programme at Key Stage 1

	Objective for talk	*Activity*
1	To become aware that there are different types of talk which are appropriate in different contexts, and that talk is learnt directly and indirectly from others.	Consider talk vocabulary. Reflect on how the capacity to engage in talk is learned. Think what sort of talk is important in group work, and why. Share ideas about talking in groupwork.
2	To understand the nature and purpose of the talk groups and to begin to build trust and confidence in the group.	Group cohesion activity to ensure that all members understand the importance of their own contribution and that of others through talk. Encouraging respect and active listening.
3	To ask questions – requesting information and reasons, and showing respect for what is offered.	Problem-solving context in which group members share their thinking in a supportive environment. Group are provided with a structure to ask for, give and consider reasons.
4	To negotiate a group agreement.	Problem-solving in which groups are required to come to a joint decision by choosing an option based on reasons provided by each other.
5	To generate and decide on a class set of ground rules for exploratory talk.	Groups suggest rules which will support effective discussion. These are contributed to a whole class discussion. Class agrees on a set of rules and agrees to implement the rules.

information. Further lessons provide opportunities to use the shared ground rules for talk, for example, to discuss problem-solving contexts generated by curriculum software or by generic software, to discuss issues with others at a distance or asynchronously, and to discuss finding and sorting relevant information from the Internet.

To illustrate these lessons further we will briefly describe a key lesson in which the set of class ground rules is generated (Dawes *et al.*, 2000). You can use this format for a range of classroom situations.

The learning objectives of the lesson are

(a) to raise children's awareness of group talk;
(b) to introduce vocabulary for talking about talk;
(c) to decide on a shared set of ground rules for talk.

The lesson begins with a whole class discussion of how people talk in different situations. The teacher introduces the idea of 'ground rules' for talk as rules which are rarely made explicit, and explains that if each member of a group is following their own different rules, it is difficult to share and discuss ideas. Groups of three then work together to define and use some key talk vocabulary. For example, they may talk about meanings and uses for words such as 'argument', 'challenge', discussion' and 'reason'. Next, the groups discuss what they think are the most important talk rules that groups might follow. They choose six rules. Finally, in a whole class plenary the class share their ideas and agree on a class set of ground rules for talking together. The teacher ensures that these rules are worded to reflect the principles for Exploratory Talk listed earlier.

The class list of ground rules for talk is displayed prominently in the classroom. Children are asked to remind one another of the rules, to put them into practice, and to evaluate their effectiveness. The succeeding Talk Lessons are designed to enable this process as the class undertake activities on and off the computer related to a range of curriculum topics.

Here is a sample of the rules for talk produced by a Year 5 class:

OUR TALKING RULES
We share our ideas and listen to each other
We talk one at a time
We respect each other's opinions
We give reasons to explain our ideas
If we disagree we ask 'why?'
We try to agree in the end

The class is asked to recall the rules before group activity at the computer.

After creating and agreeing to use the ground rules, children undertake further lessons which provide opportunities to apply and practice their new

What do you think?	*Why do you think that?*
I agree with.......... because.........	I challenge what ....says, because.........
Any more ideas to share?	Do we all agree (or shall we talk more?)

Figure 2.2 Examples of Cue Cards for Key Stage 1 Thinking Together.

skills. For example, groups are asked to consider a story or narrative in which characters may create conflict and which has a 'cliff-hanger' ending. Their task is to discuss the choices each character has at this point in the narrative, and go on to decide on their own version of a story ending. To support their learning of talk skills, Key Stage 1 children are provided with Cue Cards. (Figure 2.2) These are passed round from child to child as 'reminders' of the sort of language which can be used to find out what other people think. Groups graduate to discussing their work without such support.

Talk Lesson plans

The plan for each lesson sets out particular learning objectives for the children's talk. As each lesson starts, the teacher focuses the class attention on these and stresses that any reading, writing or drawing is incidental. Everyone is aware that they must concentrate their greatest efforts on the way they discuss things.

Each lesson has three main sections:

Whole class work 1 – in which the teacher

- explains the talk and curricular aims of the lesson;
- talks about the main themes with the class;
- sets up the group work session.

Group work – in which the children work together on an activity in their 'Talk groups'; the teacher intervenes to

- support and reinforce incipient exploratory talk episodes;
- help the children to scaffold one another's uses of the talk rules and structures;
- ensures that talk is inclusive and on task;
- model exploratory talk.

Whole class work 2 – a closing plenary in which the teacher

- enables the groups to share their work with the class;
- leads a class discussion to draw out the main points that have emerged, for example, what has been learnt and how it was learnt;
- reviews the talk aims for the lesson with the class to consider if they have been fulfilled; are the ground rules helpful? Should they be revised?

Some Thinking Together strategies for teaching and learning

We have found that the effectiveness of teaching Thinking Together varies a great deal depending on the approach of individual teachers. Those children who gained most in terms of ability to discuss ideas were in the classes of teachers who:

(i) made the aims for each lesson clear;
(ii) encouraged children to use their ground rules for talk once these had been created and agreed;
(iii) 'modelled' the kinds of language they wished to hear. For example, teachers used the whole class sessions to ask 'Why?' and 'How?' questions which provided examples of how this can help make thinking explicit to others.
(iv) used questions not just to test children on specific items of knowledge, but used a series of related questions to lead the class through a line of reasoning. This 'guided reporting' (Gibbons, 2000) is a common feature of classrooms – the teacher elicits a response from a child, then asks others to build on this contribution in a way that helps the entire class to come to a joint understanding of a topic. This way of provoking discussion through targeted questioning and active listening is a strategy children can usefully learn and subsequently offer to one another when working without teacher support in a small group.
(v) helped children to recognise and value the language and reasoning skills they are developing. For example, children can consider whether using the ground rules is changing how they talk and work together; and what benefits they perceive.

Software design and Thinking Together

So far in this chapter we have focused on Talk Lessons and not specifically on how these affect the use of ICT. The lessons prepare children for working together at the computer and create a climate of collaborative inquiry whatever the activity. However, as you will be aware, the quality of the software is crucially important if it is to support meaningful discussion and help to develop children's thinking.

We investigated what sort of software could support Exploratory Talk through an analysis of many hours of video recording of groups working at computers. We identified examples of Exploratory Talk (such as asking probing questions or giving reasons for opinions) and analysed the impact of the software on supporting or inhibiting this kind of talk. This detailed examination revealed some interface design features that seemed more effective than others in supporting Exploratory Talk. When choosing software that supports discussion, look for programmes that:

- put evidence which can be used in reasoning about choices clearly on the screen where children can point to it;
- present choices embedded in a motivating narrative;
- make problems sufficiently complex to benefit from being analysed through reflection and discussion;
- use a simple interface with multiple choice options rather than typed input;
- avoid any encouragement towards turn-taking, for example, not using discrete serial problems;
- avoid contexts in which children are asked to work against the clock.

A simple test of these ideas

An example of software that can improve the quality of thinking and learning when children are using computers is the Kate's Choice programme described earlier, which was created to co-ordinate with the citizenship curriculum. This software provides meaningful open-ended problems for discussion. Screen prompts reminded the groups to talk together before deciding what to do. As previously mentioned, before the Talk Lessons the focus group of children barely discussed the issues even when the software explicitly prompted them to do so.

In the following sequence a group of three Year 5 children (aged 8 and 9 years) are working together on the Kate's Choice software (see Figure 2.1). They are faced with the same dilemma described earlier. Before the Talk Lessons, all the groups of Year 5 children to whom we gave this software answered 'Tells her parents' with little pause for thought. After the educational programme, the children spent significantly longer talking about what to do. The following Sequence shows how Kylie, Jen and Gary arrived at their decision.

Sequence 2.2 Even though he is her friend

KYLIE: What do you think?
JEN: What do you think?
GARY: I think even though he is her friend then um she shouldn't tell of him because em well she should tell of him em because was, was, if he's stealing it it's not worth having a friend that steals is it?
KYLIE: No.
JEN: Why? I don't agree.
KYLIE: We said why?
KYLIE: I think that one as well do you?
GARY: I think she should tell her parents. Do you?
KYLIE: I think I'm I think even though he is her friend because he's stealing she should still tell her parents and her parents might give her the money and she she might be able to go to the shop and give them the money.
JEN: I think um/
GARY: /but then she's paying for the thing she stole so I think he should get {the money anyway. He should have his=
JEN: {I think that he should go and tell his mother/...
GARY: =own money Mum.
KYLIE: .../even though she has promised.
JEN: Because he's...well you shouldn't break a promise really should you
GARY: What's it worth having a friend if he's going to steal?
KYLIE: If he steals...If you know he's stolen if she don't tell her parents then he will be getting away with it.
GARY: It's not worth having a friend that steals is it?
[3-second pause]
JEN: OK then.
KYLIE: Ain't worth it is it?
JEN: Tells her parents.
GARY: Yeh go on.

The discussion shows the children considering some of the issues involved. They ask for one another's ideas and reasons, and are prepared to listen and change their minds. There is a lack of haste and a focus on thinking of alternatives in this discussion. This is not a perfect debate by any means; these children can be thought of as 'novices' in their use of discussion to resolve a dilemma. Their school's catchment area was characterised as of low socio-economic status. A high proportion (approximately one-third) of the children in the class had been granted statements of Special Need in Education for a range of emotional, behavioural and learning difficulties. This particular group had found it very difficult to work together at the beginning of the talking lessons. In this transcript it is noticeable that the children are not afraid to challenge each other and that they respond to challenges with reasons and reflection. This is very different from their behaviour before the 'Talk Lessons' when challenges led to aggression. We found that children who had not undertaken talk training ignored the screen prompts and carried on rapidly to the next screen. But the talk-focused children sat back from the screen and very deliberately solicited one another's views. Using the structure provided by the ground rules appears to help them to think about the issues of stealing and friendship more deeply, to share their thoughts, and to arrive at a joint decision. Their work at the computer was therefore much more productive and satisfying. Our research has shown that software can offer children exciting and motivating opportunities to engage in meaningful and purposeful dialogues with others. However the potential of the child and the machine may be diminished if the child's talk skills are undeveloped (Wegerif, 1996).

Summary

Children may have little idea of how to discuss their ideas effectively. We advocate preparing children for working together at computers with a series of Talk Lessons. Through these lessons classes establish shared ground rules for collaboration such as listening with respect, responding to challenges with reasons, encouraging partners to give their views and trying to reach agreement. Evidence shows that Talk Lessons can transform the quality of group work at the computer.

3

THINKING TOGETHER

In the chapter, we aim to show that teaching children how to talk together is a way of helping them to think more effectively; and that children can be taught to think together more effectively. Examples of small groups solving problems together show the importance of social relationships in the process of learning.[1]

Conversations are all different. At first glance there is little in common between conversations about babies in a group of new parents and those conversations that occur within the small groups that often gather around open car-bonnets. In the first type of conversation, it seems to be important to be very positive about other people's babies. In the second type of conversation, at least in our experience, critical comments are fine but it helps if you can show that you know your tappets from your torque wrenches.

However, conversations can share similarities. One of the reasons that new parents often like to talk to other new parents is to consider solutions to problems that they have with the care of their babies. Groups gathered around an open car-bonnet are usually also concerned to solve a problem but of a more mechanical kind. Some common strategies are likely to be useful in both situations. Open questions are useful for getting at what the problem really is. More specific questions are then needed to establish clear, shared understanding ('When you say the *thingy* do you mean the blue *thingy* or the red *thingy*?'). It is also useful in such contexts to be able to challenge ideas if you have a good reason. If a range of options are shared and evaluated, the final decision is more likely to be the best one. However, if participants are going to be able to challenge each other's ideas and offer alternatives, they need to feel confident that their challenge will be taken in the right spirit and not lead to conflict. Perhaps all the joking that goes on in conversations in both contexts serves the useful purpose of keeping the group working constructively together. Nothing unifies a group quite so effectively as shared laughter.

Individual thinking

This book stresses the value of effective group work when undertaking computer-based activities. That is, we advocate people thinking together as an important additional strategy to add to their repertoire, rather than being confined to thinking on their own. But not everyone finds it easy to work in groups; indeed many very bright and creative people seem to work best on their own. The philosopher Ludwig Wittgenstein was a good example of this. He used to retreat to an isolated hut in the wilderness to do his thinking. Those who champion individual thinking against group thinking claim, reasonably enough, that thinking is something private that happens inside an individual's brain. In this argument, dialogues with others are not indicators of joint thinking; they are at best opportunities for individuals to share their thoughts with others and perhaps to be stimulated by the thoughts of others. Thinking, in this view of things, remains stubbornly trapped inside each separate person's brain.

There is no question that people can think very clearly on their own. Encouraging the ability to think individually is rightly seen as a primary aim of education. But what does it really mean to think on one's own? People are not born with the language capacity to think on their own; we have to learn language and thinking by being drawn into thinking with others through conversations. However good individuals become at thinking alone, they rarely stop thinking with others in a range of contexts. How creative, productive or satisfying these learning dialogues are may depend on the individual's capacity to take part in them. There are simple skills, like listening to others and explicitly valuing their comments, that can expand the capacity to participate in learning dialogues.

If anyone could think for themselves it was Wittgenstein. For many philosophers, he is seen as the archetypal thinker, in fact an all-round genius. So how did Wittgenstein think on his own? His deep thoughts, as he recorded them in his diary, were essentially dialogues (Monk, 1991). He argued endlessly in his own head. He reserved his most vehement arguments for himself, attacking positions that he used to hold. One of his most profound and influential thought discoveries was that thinking itself was not really private at all. Conscious thinking depends upon language and language is never private because it is always part of a dialogue. Perhaps it is not a co-incidence that Wittgenstein, seen by many as the archetypal thinker, was born into a large family of talkative intellectuals and artists. It is unlikely that he was short of interesting conversations as he grew up. He was born in Vienna at the turn of the century, a time and a place noted for its intellectual ferment and its brilliant conversations. Nobody learns to think on their own, not even a great thinker.

The example of Wittgenstein suggests that the more originally and powerfully you can think as an individual, the more you can contribute to the larger conversations in which your thinking occurs. But how do we learn to think as individuals in the first place? The best evidence is that we learn through being drawn into conversations with others, at first through non-verbal responsive play and then through the interchange of noises, signs and recognisable words. By being drawn into conversations children learn various strategies for verbal communication, including how to take positions and argue for their own point of view.

This understanding of the role of language in thought was originally suggested by the Russian psychologist and educator, Lev Vygotsky. Vygotsky wrote that 'all that is internal in the higher mental functions was at one time external' (Vygotsky, 1991). His claim is that the intellectual performance of an individual may have its roots in their prior social experience. More precisely, he argued that psychological capacities are created by the 'internalisation' of social activity. For example, he argues that the process of silent reflection is an internalised version of talk, by which the individual can conduct an inner dialogue.

Learning to think

We all learn to think but some seem to learn better than others. If we combine Vygotsky's idea of internalisation with the idea that some dialogues are more intelligent than others, we have a sketch for a theory of how children learn to reason, and for how they might be taught to reason more effectively. That is, by participating in reasoning dialogues with others, children are learning a good way to think rationally when reflecting alone. If this account is correct, then it follows that teaching children the ground rules for effective dialogue with others should lead them to reason more effectively on their own. If they learn to reason more effectively on their own, this should be apparent in their performance in certain relevant contexts – such as how well they do in standardised tests of reasoning.

The Thinking Together research team designed an investigation to test this theory in the classroom. In carrying out the investigation, we used a reasoning test that has been widely accepted as measuring individual, non-verbal, 'context-free' reasoning: the Raven's Standard Progressive Matrices.[2] In the psychometric tradition of psychology, general intelligence is described as a factor that underlies performance on a range of tests referred to as 'g'. If only one test is to be used the Raven's Progressive Matrix is the one that is known to produce results closest to pure 'g' (Styles, 1999). This made Raven's the ideal test for our purpose. Examples of the test can be found in Raven *et al.* (1998). Raven's tests consist of a grid or matrix of abstract figures in which the children have to discover the pattern in order to complete the matrix.

Our hypothesis was that individual performance on reasoning tests was at least in part a product of the internalisation of a type of conversation or dialogue. The test we devised using Raven's would show that, if our hypothesis was true, we should be able to improve children's individual results on the Raven's test simply by teaching them to follow the social ground rules of intelligent conversations. The social ground rules of intelligent conversations that we taught were the ground rules of Exploratory Talk described in Chapter 2.

Measuring group reasoning and individual changes

In one Thinking Together research project we taught Talk Lessons to three target classes of children (aged 9 and 10). Children were encouraged to use and reflect on the ground rules for collective reasoning. The lessons did not include any activities or strategies for solving abstract reasoning test problems. Nevertheless, we investigated the impact of this intervention on reasoning by providing two versions of the Raven's non-verbal reasoning test; one which children completed in groups of three, and the other which they undertook alone. These tests were given to the children before the Talk Lessons programme began and again afterwards (around twelve weeks later) so that we could compare their reasoning on the same problems. We also gave the same tests twelve weeks apart to three matched classes in other similar schools, who thus served as a 'control'. We found that the groups in the experimental classes did much better afterwards than they had done beforehand.

It is not perhaps very surprising that children who were taught the ground rules of Exploratory Talk did better at solving the Raven's problems in groups than those in control classes who had not been taught to use these ground rules. What is more surprising is that these same 'target' children also improved their test performances as individuals. The statistically significant results of these tests showed not only that the groups in the classes which we taught improved their scores on the test by about 10 per cent but also that the same children working on their own using a similar test increased their individual scores more than the control children. In comparison, children in the control classes showed no significant increase (Mercer *et al.*, 1999). This finding has since been confirmed by two further studies: in Mexico and elsewhere in the United Kingdom.

The outcome of this research appears to confirm the hypothesis that reasoning ability can be improved by teaching children the ground rules for intelligent conversations. It also appears to support the Vygotskian theoretical claim that individual thinking is shaped by the internalisation of social communication.

How did the children learn to think better?

It was pleasing to have confirmation of the link between language use and the development of reasoning ability. Further interesting findings were provided by analysis of the transcripts of video recordings which revealed exactly how the social ground rules that we taught, the kind of conversation, helped the children to think together. As part of the study we video-recorded groups working together to undertake the Raven's reasoning tests, both before and after the Talk Lessons. This meant that we could consider the talk of the same group of children working on the same problem before and after the Talk Lessons. We could compare their initial discussion before the Talk Lessons, when they failed to solve the problem, with the more successful discussion afterwards when they achieved the correct solution. That is, we were able to make a detailed comparison of more and less *intelligent* conversations.

The next section of this chapter discusses the implications of three of these 'before and after' examples of children's talk.

Example 1: Distributed cognition

Sequence 3.1, 'No, because' and Sequence 3.2, 'That goes out look', involve Elaine, John and Liam (aged 9 and 10 years). In the first sequence they are talking about a Raven's problem before the Talk Lessons intervention. In Sequence 3.2, they talk about the same problem after the Talk Lessons programme. Figure 3.1 provides the problem: it may be helpful to solve this for yourself before reading the sequences of dialogue.

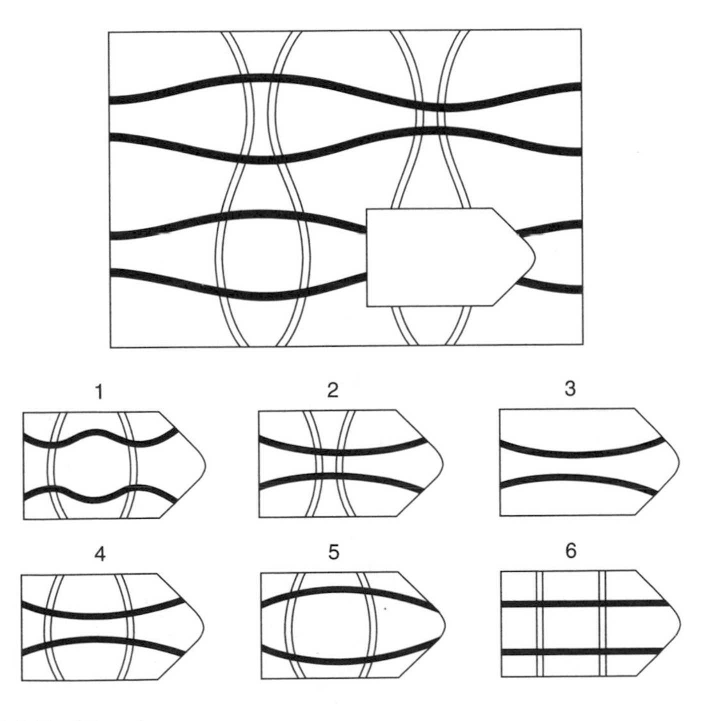

Figure 3.1 Problem A.

Sequence 3.1 No, because

ELAINE: No, because it will come along like that.
(*Elaine circles answer 5, which is not the right answer.*)

Sequence 3.2 That goes out look

JOHN: Number 5.
DANNY: I think it's number 2.
JOHN: No, it's out, that goes out look.
DANNY: Yeh but as it comes in it goes this.
ELAINE: Now we're talking about this bit so it can't be number 2 it's that one.
ELAINE: It's that one it's that one.
DANNY: Yeh 'cos look.
ELAINE: 4.
DANNY: I agree with 4.
(*John nods in assent and Elaine circles answer 4, which is correct.*)

It is interesting to consider why the group succeed in the post-test (Sequence 3.2) and fail in the pre-test (Sequence 3.1). This is one of the earlier problems in the Raven's series and one that most groups got right the first time. If you look just at the lines running vertically you might think that the answer is number 5 because that continues the pattern for these lines. This (incorrect) conclusion is that which the children reached in their initial 'pre-test' attempt. Elaine did not pause to consider alternatives or to reach agreement with her group, but circled answer 5. That she said 'because' reflects the fact that she was responding to someone else's suggestion, made through silent pointing at one of the pictures. Before the Talk Lessons, the children rushed through all the problems with little talk.

After the ten-week series of Talk Lessons, you can see that the children take more time over the problem. Their deliberations illustrate why three heads are sometimes better than one, or even two. As before, it seems that the pattern of the vertical lines is noticed and John offers number 5 as the answer. But this answer is only made as a suggestion. Danny puts forward number 2 as the answer, apparently because he is looking at the horizontal pattern. John explains (through a combination of words and pointing) that the vertical lines have to 'go out'. Danny in turn explains that it cannot be number 5 because the horizontal lines have to 'go in'. Each child has adopted a different perspective; John takes the side of the vertical lines, Danny that of the horizontal lines. Each can see enough to refute the position of the other but this does not produce the solution. Elaine, building on the discussion and the reasons given, comes up with the answer which combines the vertical lines going out with the horizontal lines going in, that is, number 4. Both Danny and John can see that she is right according to the same arguments that they have already put forward for their different positions.

These children found the solution to this problem through applying the ground rules of reasoning which they had been taught. They explored different alternatives, responding to challenges with reasons and tried to reach an agreement before moving on. We can see here directly how the ground rules helped the children to think together. The way in which these children solved the problem is a striking illustration of how dialogue can work in general to solve problems and to help us build higher levels of understanding. Because each child drew attention to a different aspect of the problem they were then able to bring their different perspectives together in formulating a more comprehensive – and more accurate – solution.

Example 2: Building language for thinking

The children in Example 1 relied heavily on non-verbal communication – pointing – to argue their positions. However, we wish to focus now on the effect of explicit verbalisation of problems. The following group, Keira, Perry and Tara, were particularly interesting for this aspect of the analysis. Before the Talk Lessons they had scored lower working together than the highest of their individual scores, whereas after the lessons they scored higher working together than the highest individual score. This result shows that they were doing better together than any of them could have done working alone. Before the Talk Lessons this group scored 39 out of 60. After their lessons they achieved 47. This meant that there were eight questions that they had failed to solve in the pre-test which they managed to solve in the post-test. Focusing on the talk around these questions enabled us to compare successful talk with unsuccessful talk for the same children about the same problems.

Sequence 3.3, 'We haven't done that', was recorded before the Talk Lessons, while Sequence 3.4, 'I think it's a number', was recorded after. Sequence 3.4 is an edited version of the groups talk around the problem as the original transcript was very long.

Sequence 3.3 We haven't done that

KEIRA: We haven't done that.
TARA: (giggles) this is where your Mum can see what you're really like at school Perry.
TARA: Square and diamond, it's 2.
PERRY: No it's not.
TARA: It is 2.
PERRY: No it's not.

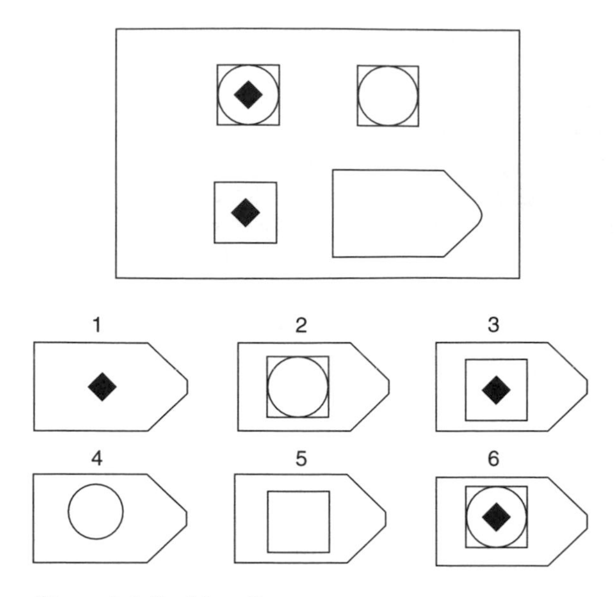

Figure 3.2 Problem B.

TARA: It is.
PERRY: No it's not.
KEIRA: It's that one 6.
TARA: It is.
PERRY: No it's not it's got to be a square and a circle.
TARA: Its that, it has to be that, it has to be that, it has to be 6 because look they've only got that (*pointing to the pictures*).
KEIRA: Look first they are starting with one of them things over (*pointing*) and then it has to be black.
PERRY: Right, 6.
KEIRA: No it isn't Perry.
TARA: That's number 2 because it goes bigger and bigger and bigger (*Tara is looking at the next question*).
KEIRA: It isn't Perry, look at that one, no it isn't Perry.
(*Perry writes '6', which is the wrong answer. Keira pushes him.*)
PERRY: Keira! All right someone else be the writer then.
KEIRA: Me (*forcibly takes paper*).
TARA: No, Keira you have to sit in this chair to be the writer (*Tara takes pen*).
TARA: Give it to Perry because he's quicker at it.
KEIRA: Give me the pen (*takes the pen*).
KEIRA: Are we finished on that one, are we on that one now.

TARA: You're not allowed to do it.
PERRY: Let Tara have a go when we get up to E.
(*Turn to next exercise*).
KEIRA: Well what do you think it is you dur brain? (*addressed to Perry*).

Sequence 3.4 I think it's number...

TARA: That has got to be a diamond, a square with a diamond with a circle in that one, number 6, do you agree?
PERRY: No, what do you mean?
TARA: OK no it's got to be square.
KEIRA: I think it's number 6, that's the one.
PERRY: No it ain't.
KEIRA: I think it's number 6.
TARA: No 'cause it's got to swing round every time, so there is a circle in it.
KEIRA: Yes but it hasn't got a circle in there has it and that one has (*indicating*).
(*3-second pause. Concentrated faces*)
KEIRA: It's that because look that's got a square so it's just got to be empty.
PERRY: With no circle in so it's just got to be an empty square.
KEIRA: No they are just normal boxes.
TARA: Look, that's got a triangle, that's got a square. Look. that's got a square with a diamond with a circle in, that's got a square with a diamond in and that's got a square with a circle in so that's got to be a square.
PERRY: I don't understand this at all.
TARA: Because, look, on that they've taken the circle out yes? So on that you are going to take the circle out because they have taken the circle out of that one.
PERRY: On this they have taken the circle out and on this they have taken the diamond out and on this they have put them both in, so it should be a blank square because look it goes circle square.
KEIRA: It's got to be a blank square. Yeh it is.
PERRY: Do you agree on number 5, do you agree on 5?
(*Perry writes '5', which is the correct answer.*)

Again you can see that the group correctly answers the question after the Talk Lessons. In the pre-intervention talk of Sequence 3.3, Perry challenges Tara's first suggestion ('it is 2') without giving a reason. Tara offers no further justification for her suggestion. This leads into a series of exchanges typical of disputational talk, in which participants simply assert their opposing views without reasoning. Keira then suggests 'It is that one 6' and this is taken up by Tara, and both she and Keira offer reasons. '6' is apparently agreed upon, and Perry writes it down. However, Keira then appears to change her mind without saying what her new opinion is (or she may be objecting to Perry writing the answer down before checking properly with herself and Tara; we do not know as no reason is made explicit). There is then a dispute about who should be writing the answers on the answer sheet.

Sequence 3.4 illustrates some ways that the talk of the same children changed. Compared with Sequence 3.3 there are more long turns taken as more elaborate explanations are given. Again, Tara is the first to propose an answer, but this time she does this not as a statement ('it is 2') but as an elaborated hypothesis with a question encouraging debate ('That has got to be a diamond, a square with a diamond with a circle in that one, number 6, do you agree?'). Perry asks for more explanation. This time his challenge prompts Tara not into a conflict but into an attempt to be more explicit. Through this effort Tara appears to see that she is wrong and changes her claim. Perry and Keira again engage in a 'disputational' exchange but this is short-lived. After a pause (for individual thought?) the children return to using language to think explicitly together about the problem. They come to agree that it is a kind of subtraction problem which they express in the form 'taking the x out of y'. They agree upon the correct answer.

You may have noticed that many features of the talk are different in this second transcript section. Explicit reasons for claims are given, challenges are offered with reasons, several alternatives are considered before a decision is reached, and the children can be seen seeking to reach agreement together. Explicit reasoning may be represented in talk by the incidence of some specific ways of using language, and we can see here some 'key features': the hypothetical nature of claims is indicated by a preceding 'I think', reasons are linked to claims by the use of 'because' or 'cause' and agreement is sought through the question 'do you agree?'. Explicit reasoning requires the linking of clauses and leads here to longer utterances.

When analysing the transcripts, we found that in less successful talk episodes 'because' commonly was used in the context of a speaker simply pointing at a physical item without making any reasoning explicit. In the more successful talk sequences, 'because' was more often used to introduce an explicit, verbalised, reason. These different ways of using 'because' are illustrated in the sequences already given.

(a) (*Unsuccessful talk. Pre-intervention*)

TARA: Its that, it has to be that, it has to be that, it has to be 6 because look they've only got that (pointing to the pictures).

(b) (*Successful talk. Post-intervention*)

TARA: Because look on that they've taken the circle out yes? So on that you are going to take the circle out because they have taken the circle out of that one.

In comparing these two ways of using *because* we see a shift in the talk from pointing to the physical context towards pointing to a verbal context which the children construct together. This shift is also reflected in a far greater number of long turns at talk being taken in the more successful talk. This construction of a shared verbal context can be seen in Perry's response to Tara's reasoning in example (b):

PERRY: On this they have taken the circle out and on this they have taken the diamond out and on this they have put them both in, so it should be a blank square because look it goes circle square.

In referring to the process of 'taking the circle out' Tara is verbalising something that cannot be pointed to directly in the picture. She is referring to a hypothetical change, one that exists only in language. Turning back to Figure 3.2 we can see that it provides a solution to the problem. Once Tara has made this relationship verbally explicit Perry is able to see it and he echoes Tara's construction. This use of language to 'model' relationships and processes was often found in the more successful talk of all the groups. Expressions such as 'the same', 'getting fatter', 'that and that make that' or 'add that to that and you get that' were all used.

Example 3: Emotional intelligence

The research data provide useful illustrations of various ways in which language can be used by children as a tool for thinking together. But the changes which took place as a result of the Talk Lessons are more than changes in the way language is used. They are also changes in the way the children relate to each other. In the final example Sequence 3.5, 'I know what it is' and Sequence 3.6, 'Wait a minute' Natalie, Jane and Liam are trying to solve the same Raven's problem (Figure 3.3) before and after the Talk Lessons.

Sequence 3.5 I know what it is

LIAM: We've only got three more to do.
JANE: I know what it is.
NATALIE: That, that.
(*circles number 3, incorrect, on the answer sheet. Sound of page turning*)

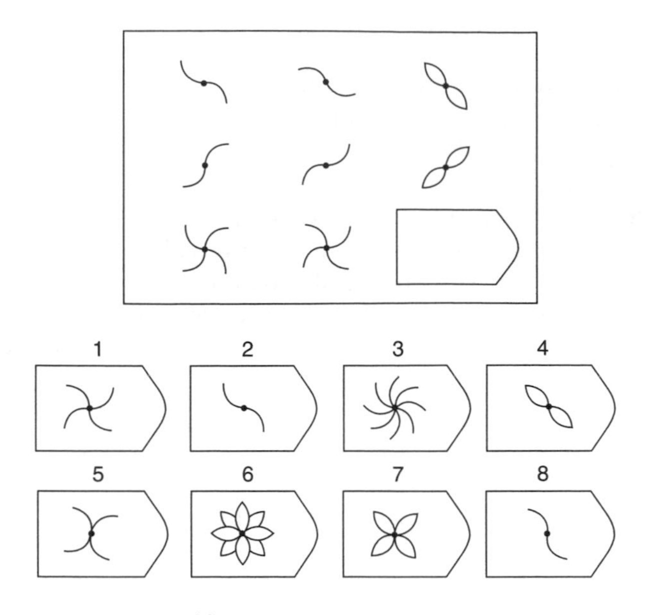

Figure 3.3 Problem C.

Sequence 3.6 Wait a minute

NATALIE: E1.
(pause)
NATALIE: Right I know. Wait a minute – look, that and that and that and that and that and that together – put it all together and what do you get you get that.
LIAM: Yeh, cos' they've all got a dot in the middle.
NATALIE: Wait a minute.
JANE: I actually think it's…
NATALIE: I think it's number 6.
LIAM: Or number 7?
NATALIE: Who agrees with me?
PERRY: No it's number 7 cos' that and that makes that. Number 7 yeh.
NATALIE: Yeh.
JANE: Number 7. E1.
(*circles number 7, correct, on the answer sheet.*)

Here a clearer use of language helps the children to solve the problem. In the first sequence they hardly talk at all. In the second, they spend slightly longer discussing it. Liam gives a reason for his view. On the video, Jane and Natalie can be seen pausing when they hear his reasoning, apparently reflecting, before agreeing with him. In addition to this, it is also interesting to evaluate the shift in relationships in the group.

In the class girls had not wanted to work with boys and when the teacher arranged them in mixed gender groups there were many complaints. Before the Talk Lessons Natalie and Jane co-operated well but agreed with each other so quickly that they did little sustained thinking. Jane offered few suggestions. Liam occasionally protested but was ignored. His disagreements were treated as disruptive and indeed at times they were. After the Talk Lessons the whole group are seen working well together. The combination of all of the children's ideas provides the critical element that the group needed to solve some of the more difficult problems. This is achieved by listening to one another better; Natalie and Jane have begun to take Liam's disagreements seriously. While in the pre-test his challenges sometimes took the form of hitting the table in the post-test they are constructive, using reasons to help take the group understanding forward. As with Tara, Perry and Keira this greater success was associated with a change in the way the group used language, especially questions which are often an important tool for group thinking. The main change was not in the direction of supporting cognition but of promoting inclusion. One of the reasons why Jane, Natalie and Liam were thinking together more effectively was because there were more invitations to contribute. Liam's inclusion was important not because he knew the answers; he did not. But his tendency to challenge meant that important alternatives were now considered before conclusions were reached. Jane and Natalie no longer accepted each other's first suggestions. All three children had developed a better capacity to initiate and sustain intelligent conversations – and in doing so were better able to 'get along together' as a group. They had realised that they could usefully state and consider a range of points of view.

What we can learn from the examples

Although solving reasoning test problems could be considered an artificial context for thinking, the dialogues that we recorded have improved our general understanding of effective group thinking. In Example 1, the children's relative lack of success in their pre-intervention talk seems to be because they each have a limited view. You can picture their problem; it is like that described in the traditional Islamic folk story 'The Elephant and the Blind Men'.[3] A wealthy king once wanted to make a point to his quarrelling counsellors. He brought a group of blind men to the palace courtyard and asked them to describe what they found. In the courtyard was an elephant, at that time a great novelty in the kingdom. The first blind man, finding the elephant's trunk, decided that this was an animal like a snake. The next, who had come up against a leg, disagreed with the first man saying that it was an animal shaped like a tree. The third felt part of an ear and so rejected what the other two had said, claiming that in fact this animal was more like a ship's sail. Finding the tail, the fourth was certain the animal was like a rope. The king pointed out to his disputational counsellors that each man could be right. And yet all were wrong, because they were each arguing from a limited perspective with no idea what the whole elephant might be like. Sharing their information would have helped all of them to understand better.

At first Elaine, John and Danny failed to solve the first Raven's problem because only an initial individual perspective was taken into account; the view of Elaine who saw part of the puzzle and was holding the pencil. When asked to solve the same puzzle after having Talk Lessons the group tried to reconcile several different individual perspectives through talking together. This led them to see how each individual bit of the pattern fitted into a more complex whole.

This example is relevant to a consideration of the features of successful and unsuccessful collective thinking in general. We may seize on just one aspect of complex problems, hanging onto a little truth instead of going on to see the larger picture. To move forward it is often necessary to listen carefully to alternative perspectives and to be prepared to let go of our initial impression. For individuals this requires both the intellectual humility to doubt your convictions and the emotional confidence to 'let go' of your initial ideas. Both this kind of 'humility' and this kind of 'confidence' are, we suggest, a product of shared ground rules in exploratory discussion.

In Example 2, Tara, Perry and Keira eventually find a solution by using language to model hypothetical changes in the Raven's patterns. As in the first example, they begin by pointing at what they can see directly in the picture but this does not provide the answer. They then use language to describe imaginary manipulations of the image, 'swinging things round', 'taking things out' and so on. This verbal modelling enables them to discover a relationship that they could not point to directly on the page. We suggest that learning to solve reasoning test problems of even a 'non-verbal' test like the Raven's will involve a shift from a perceptual level of reasoning, pointing to things on the page, to verbal reasoning. Language not only enables experience to be represented and shared, it allows invisible, hypothetical processes and factors to be offered towards a communal pool of ideas.

Tara, Perry and Keira could use language to build new understandings because of a shift in the way in which they related to each other. The Talk Lessons did not teach the children how to recognise concepts such as 'subtraction', only ground rules such as listening with respect and responding to challenges with reasons. When, for example, they asked what one another thought, and if they all agreed, they were implicitly referring back to lessons in which these ground rules had been emphasised. Commendably, these children show a mix of 'humility' and 'confidence' in action.

This social and emotional dimension to group thinking is brought out even more clearly in the third example. Initially Natalie, Jane and Liam did not work well together, but through their use of the ground rules they became an effective team. This example shows that the emotional sensitivity and positive affect required for good group work can be influenced by teaching. These personal feelings are shaped by the social environment and particularly by the ways in which people talk to each other. Through the simple technique of asking and listening to answers Natalie, Perry and Jane turned from acting like opponents to acting as collaborators. Interviews with children involved in the programme show that this apparent increase in friendly behaviour is often reflected in changes in the way that they feel about each other.

Listening to and including others who are different from ourselves (and most people are) can sound like an ethical injunction asking for some sort of self-sacrifice. Many practically minded people object to this kind of demand on the grounds that it is not efficient or effective. The example of Natalie, Jane and Liam shows that including awkward others may not only be an ethical demand but can also be a way of improving the effectiveness of group thinking. The idea that intelligent problem-solving is linked to the ability to work well in group settings can be related to the currently popular notion of 'emotional intelligence' (Goleman, 1996). The study we have reported suggests that 'intelligent emotions' are found first in 'intelligent conversations' and can then be acquired by individuals. Intelligent emotions are intelligent precisely because they open up the possibilities of shared thinking instead of closing them down.

The implications of these findings

Witnessing groups of children solving Raven's tests provides examples of collaborative thinking. But after the talk lessons children did better even on individual tests of reasoning. Experience of the collective or 'dialogical' thinking promoted through the Talk Lessons seemed to influence the quality of individual reasoning. From this evidence it seems that at least part of what is meant by 'intelligence' is forged in intelligent conversations. Teachers can enlist the tools that ICT offers to help children develop their capacity to participate in such learning dialogues. The implications for the design of teaching and learning activities are considered in the rest of this book.

Summary

Learning dialogues can translate into enhanced thinking skills. Some ground rules followed by participants in dialogues have good results for the quality of their shared problem-solving while other ground rules can have a negative impact. The effectiveness of the ground rules for Exploratory Talk described in Chapter 2 was tested by looking at the difference that following these rules made to groups solving problems together. The reasoning problems used were abstract picture-based problems designed to measure the 'non-verbal reasoning ability' of individual children independent of confusing linguistic and cultural variables. Using the ground rules helped groups solve these kind of problems better. In addition, using the ground rules led children to think more effectively even when working on their own.

Some dialogues can be considered to be more generally intelligent than others. These are the kind of learning dialogues that the Thinking Together approach seeks to promote around computers. Extracts of transcripts can show the value of combining perspectives, how language can become a tool for joint thinking and how the ground rules for exploratory talk enable children to work collaboratively. Children can learn how to reason better by being encouraged to use Exploratory Talk. This has important consequences for understanding the best way to integrate computers into classroom practice. Computer-based activities that support learning dialogues can integrate thinking skills into the curriculum.

4

THINKING SKILLS AND ICT

Claims that there is a direct link between the use of computers and learning are examined in this chapter. In particular, the influential claims of Seymour Papert the developer of LOGO, about the value of computers are discussed in the light of evidence concerning the social dimension of learning, and the crucial role of teachers.

Seymour Papert beams at the world from his web site; he has much to look pleased about. His site recounts how Papert was ridiculed in the early days when he claimed that personal computers had the potential to transform education, then goes on to list Papert's many triumphs. These include the fact that LOGO, the logic-based programming language for children that he helped to develop and then championed, is currently used in all UK schools. In his influential book, *Mindstorms: Children, Computers and Powerful Ideas*, Papert criticised the use of computers for drill and practice exercises, and argued in favour of the value of using computers as a tool for general intellectual development (Papert, 1981). His approach, he wrote, was about allowing the kids to programme the computers, not letting the computers programme the kids.

Early in his career, Papert researched the development of mathematical reason with the Swiss psychologist Jean Piaget who is often referred to as 'the father of constructivism' in modern education. In essence, constructivism is the claim that children do not simply absorb knowledge passively when teachers tell them things but that learning proceeds actively as they construct meaning for themselves. For constructivists learning occurs when children build theories and models to explain experience. In his introduction to *Mindstorms* Papert offers an example from his own life to illustrate his view of the potential role of computers as a constructivist learning tool. He describes how a fascination with mechanical gears as a young child gave him a concrete way to understand and visualise all kinds of mathematical functions from multiplication to differentiation. Playing with gears, he claims, laid the foundation for his later career as a mathematician. Just like the gear set he had as a child, he believes that computers can be used to give complex abstract ideas a concrete form that can be manipulated by children. But since computers are massively more flexible their power lies in offering children a huge range of resources with which to develop their minds.

Papert's brand of constructivism has been very influential in the field of educational computing. Most writers about educational software since *Mindstorms* accept Papert's distinction between the computer used as a teaching machine and the computer used as a tool to help learners construct meaning for themselves. Most also seem to accept his valuation that only open-ended constructivist software of this kind can support general intellectual development or the learning of general thinking skills. But are these assumptions justified? Papert's vision of children learning by programming computers seems to neglect the role of teachers, schools and interaction with other learners.

This chapter reviews some of the different ways in which ICT has been used to support the teaching and learning of general thinking skills. Evidence from studies of these ways of using computers will help to assess the extent to which Papert was justified and to what extent his views might benefit from modification.

What are thinking skills?

The list of thinking skills specified in the English National Curriculum is similar to many such lists. It includes:

- information-processing;
- reasoning;
- enquiry;
- creative thinking;
- evaluation.

While some approaches to teaching thinking treat such skills as separate, other approaches treat them all as aspects of high quality thinking or 'higher order thinking'. Higher order thinking can be considered as complex thinking that requires effort and produces valued outcomes. Its outcomes are not predictable because the process of higher order thinking is not mechanical. This makes higher order thinking hard to define. Nonetheless, it is possible to recognise higher order thinking and to teach it (Resnick, 1987).

It may not be possible to specify what are universal thinking skills or to describe generalisable strategies for learning and problem-solving. However, it is widely accepted that there is a range of relatively general learning strategies that can be drawn out of some contexts and applied again in new contexts (Claxton, 1999). Most approaches to teaching thinking do not focus narrowly on procedural skills. Successful thinking skills programmes seem to promote a variety of apparently quite different kinds of attributes including strategies, habits, attitudes, emotions, motivations, aspects of character or self-identity and also engagement in dialogue and in a community of enquiry. These thinking skills are not united by any single psychological theory. But they are all things that practitioners believe can and should be taught or encouraged in order to improve the perceived quality and effectiveness of children's thinking.

Mindtools

The approach to computing advocated by Papert is summed up in the use of the term 'mindtools'. This term is defined by Jonassen as follows:

> Mindtools are computer applications that, when used by learners to represent what they know, necessarily engage them in critical thinking about the content they are studying. Mindtools scaffold different forms of reasoning about content. That is, they require students to think about what they know in different, meaningful ways. For instance, using databases to organise students' understanding of content organisation necessarily engages them in analytical reasoning, where creating an expert system rule base requires them to think about the causal relationships between ideas. Students cannot use Mindtools as learning strategies without thinking deeply about what they are studying.
>
> (Jonassen, 2000)

The main idea is not that computers will directly teach thinking but that, through working with computers, the student will be encouraged to think logically and by doing so will acquire internal cognitive tools for their own later use in other contexts.

Programming is a good example of the use of computers as a mindtool in this sense. Some of the general thinking skills that have been claimed to result from programming include the following:

- Learning problem-solving, problem-finding and problem-management strategies such as breaking a problem into parts or relating it to a previously solved problem.
- Learning how to plan and to undertake the kind of diagnostic thinking involved in debugging.
- Practising formal reasoning and representation such as thinking of all possible combinations, and constructing mathematical models.

- Valuing positive cognitive styles such as precision.
- Emphasising a reflective approach over an impulsive approach.
- Reinforcing attributes such as persistence and enthusiasm for meaningful academic engagement. (Adapted from Perkins and Salomon, 1989.)

Children who learn to program probably do have to learn to use at least some of these skills and attitudes. But it does not follow that skills they learn in the context of programming will transfer to be useful to them in other situations. Since the publication of *Mindstorms* in 1980 the logic-based programming language LOGO, promoted by Papert, has been widely used and evaluated in schools around the world. There is no evidence that its use has led to any dramatic increase in abstract thinking or general thinking ability. Research suggests that working with LOGO does not in itself automatically produce any general thinking skills that transfer to uses in other contexts. The evidence is rather that this kind of transfer only occurs when teachers plan activities and experiences that help to make it happen (Hughes, 1990).

In the light of this evidence, it is useful to consider what sort of teaching can make LOGO work as a support for teaching general thinking skills within the curriculum. Based on experiments with different ways of teaching with LOGO the prominent Belgian educationalist, Erik de Corte, proposed the following set of conditions which favour the teaching and learning of transferable thinking skills. De Corte (1990) describes these as *features of powerful learning environments*:

- Learners need an explicit explanation of the cognitive components of the task (a 'thinking' vocabulary).
- Learners need to observe an expert performing the task (modelling).
- Learners need to be given hints and feedback on their own performance (coaching).
- Learners need to be given direct support in the early stages of learning a task (scaffolding) and to move gradually towards self-regulation and autonomy (teacher-fading).
- Learners need the opportunity to articulate their cognitive and metacognitive strategies and to make comparisons with other learners (reflection).
- Learners need to explore, identify and define new problems in a domain and be shown how strategies acquired in one domain can be used to solve problems in another domain (transfer).

Using LOGO, on its own, does not teach children anything apart from how to use LOGO. But the activity of programming in LOGO could be a resource for teachers who aim to lead students towards the goal of acquiring transferable thinking skills. The combination of elements required for this, according to Erik de Corte, includes whole class dialogues, in which the teacher shares thinking aims and a thinking vocabulary, and small group dialogues in which children have a chance to articulate and so take ownership of new general thinking strategies.

An example of an ICT lesson applying some of these principles

We applied many of the general principles outlined by Erik de Corte using the Thinking Together approach to teach programming a robotic roamer to a class of 6-year-old children. The aim of this activity was to teach the transferable skill of writing a clear set of instructions. The difficulty of writing clear instructions, the sort of instructions that could be followed by anyone anywhere, lies in abstracting from experience only the essential elements that are required to achieve a task. Robots are excellent partners for this training exercise in abstract thinking because they really do know nothing other than what the children tell them. The lesson began with a whole class exercise in which the link between giving clear instructions and programming a robot was made through giving volunteer children wearing blindfolds instructions as to how to move around the room. The children were asked to do nothing other than what they were told to, so unless they were told to stop they would keep walking until they hit the wall. This dramatises in an amusing way the need for absolutely explicit and context-free instructions.

In preparation, the ground rules for Exploratory Talk and Thinking Together vocabulary were rehearsed by the teacher who also modelled the use of 'because' to give reasons in response to a challenge or disagreement. Then the children were asked to work in groups, applying the ground rules to devise a program or set of instructions that would send the roamer around a specific route on a large floor mat. Discussion helped the groups to achieve this task, challenging and correcting each other's ideas of what to put in the programme. Each set of instructions was tested by another group using a toy car on the map before using the roamer. The small group work developing and testing programmes gave children the opportunity to articulate and understand the central idea of generating explicit instructions that were both sufficient and precise. In the groups' discussions the general thinking skills embodied in Exploratory Talk were applied to develop aspects of thinking appropriate to computer programming. In a follow-up activity, the same general principles were applied to writing clear directions for visiting different shops using a map of a town. In the closing plenary, the teacher emphasised the general principles involved in writing a clear set of instructions and so made a bridge between the two contexts of programming the roamer and writing directions for others to follow using a map.

Visualisations and simulations

There is more to the idea of 'mindtools' than just programming in LOGO. Representations of every kind are also a mindtool that allow us to objectify our thoughts so that we can reflect upon them. Writing, graphs, tables and specialist notations such as mathematics are cognitive tools allowing thought to leap-frog to a higher level of understanding. Computers can help learners capitalise on this by allowing the direct manipulation of representations. Doing so can provide instant feedback on the implications of any changes made. Many ideas that are not obvious when written down or represented in static images become easy to grasp when converted into an interactive simulation. The phases of the moon is one example; the functioning of the cardio-vascular system another.

It is relatively uncontroversial to consider that visualisations and simulations, when well constructed, may help us to think better about an area. However, the literature about using the computer as a tool sometimes blurs the distinction between using external cognitive tools, for example, computers, and developing internal cognitive tools, or thinking skills. These are not the same things. For example, using a calculator may be a cognitive tool in the sense that it helps with long division but this does not help children know how to do long division when they forget their calculator. In the same way using computers as an external tool does not necessarily produce any internal cognitive tools that children can take away with them. Whether or not it will do so depends very much on the design of the software and the role of the teacher.

Constructivists may tend to exaggerate the educational benefits of building things with computers. Jonassen (2000), for example, claims that the best way to learn about an area is to build a computer system to model the area. However, experience of building computer systems would suggest that far more time is spent learning how to use specific computer tools effectively than in direct learning about any area. Building simulations may offer something new but ultimately is not a very efficient approach to teaching and learning about subject areas.

Concept mapping

Concept maps or 'semantic networks' are spatial representations of concepts and their interrelationships. Some writers claim that concept maps can be used to represent the knowledge structures that humans store in their minds (Jonassen, 2000). While concept maps do not require computers, computer-based concept-mapping software, such as SemNet, Learning Tool, Inspiration, Mind Mapper and many others facilitate the production of clear, easily modified concept maps. Strong claims are made for the use of concept mapping as a tool to support critical thinking and reflection on the organisation of knowledge in a subject area while also learning about the area (Buzan and Buzan, 2000; Jonassen, 2000). Here is what Jonassen and colleagues say about them:

> The purpose of semantic networks is to represent the structure of knowledge that someone has constructed. So, creating semantic networks requires learners to analyse the structural relationships among the content they are studying. By comparing semantic networks created at different points in time, they can also be used as evaluation tools for assessing changes in thinking by learners.
>
> (Jonassen *et al.*, 1998)

Concept maps have been used to support inquiry-based science and claims have been made that concept mapping is especially suited to science education (Scanlon *et al.*, 1996). Some research conducted in Canada suggests that the benefits of concept mapping can be greatly enhanced if they are used as a focus for collaborative learning (Roth, 1994; Roth and Roychoudhury, 1994).

Teachers Kerry Rich and Rachel Briggs used computer-based concept maps and the Thinking Together approach with a Year 4 class (8-year olds) in their primary school in North Tyneside (Higgins, 2003). The children, working in groups of three in a computer lab, were encouraged to make connections between twelve objects on screen, and to use the mapping tools in *Kidspiration* to create visual links to organise their ideas. This software enables the children to move between the visual diagrams to a writing view where they can expand upon their ideas and give reasons for their links. It helped that children in the study were already familiar with the format of the software having previously used its tools to create an explanation text to illustrate the life cycle of a duck. The children revised their ground rules for talk and then spent thirty minutes in discussion to make the relevant links between objects on the screen. The use of this ICT-based activity stimulated a great deal of Exploratory Talk as children realised that there were different but still reasonable ways to link things. Here are some examples:

Claim: 'The calculator and the phone are linked because they've both got buttons.'

Counter-challenge: 'But what about the clock, the phone and the calculator as they all have numbers?'

Creative reasoning: 'The clock and the egg-box are linked because the clock has twelve numbers on it, and the egg-box has twelve eggs in it.'

Hypermedia (e.g. building web sites)

Designing multimedia products such as web sites is a complex process that engages many skills. The thinking skills that learners require as designers of multimedia presentations have been listed as:

Project management skills

- Creating a timeline for the completion of the project.
- Allocating resources and time to different parts of the project.
- Assigning roles to team members.

Research skills

- Determining the nature of the problem and how research should be organised.
- Posing thoughtful questions about structure, models, cases, values and roles.
- Searching for information using text, electronic and pictorial information sources.
- Developing new information with interviews, questionnaires and other survey methods.
- Analysing and interpreting all the information collected to identify and interpret patterns.

Organisational and representation skills

- Deciding how to segment and sequence information to make it understandable.
- Deciding how information will be represented (text, pictures, movies, audio, etc.).
- Deciding how the information will be organised (hierarchy, sequence) and how it will be linked.

Presentation skills

- Mapping the design on to the presentation and implementing the ideas in multimedia.
- Attracting and maintaining the interests of the intended audiences.

Reflection skills

- Evaluating the program and the process used to create it.
- Revising the design of the program using feedback.

(Carver *et al.*, 1992)

An analysis of these skills indicates that many of them depend on the ability to work effectively with other people. The advantages of hypermedia over say, designing a poster display, are that it can provide stimulating and engaging contexts, allow access to a wealth of information and resources, and can help learners to generate high quality products to share with a range of audiences. Designing multimedia might well support the teaching of transferable thinking skills. But in order for this to happen, the learner's understanding of the development in their own thinking, talking and social skills must be emphasised as a primary purpose of the work. That is, an awareness of *how* the project was undertaken is as valuable a product as the multimedia end result. The learner's involvement in the purposes and processes of their own learning is essential.

Computer games

It has been argued that playing computer games can help develop general thinking skills. For example, the game Lemmings, often considered purely as an entertainment game, may have the potential to develop skills such as the following:

- understanding and representing the problem (including identifying what kinds of information are relevant to its solution);
- gathering and organising relevant information;
- constructing and managing a plan of action, or a strategy;
- reasoning, hypothesis-testing and decision-making;
- using various problem-solving tools.

(Whitebread, 1997)

However the game can be played with equal enjoyment and verve when the problems it poses are not understood, relevant information is not considered, no strategies are generated, and trial and error is the only way of testing ideas. While game players may learn to play a particular game and in doing so learn how other games 'work' there is no guarantee that they will make the leap of transferring this understanding to off-game experiences and situations.

However, collaboration around games seems to have a positive effect on children's ability to solve problems. One research finding is that when groups of children played the problem-solving game *The Incredible Machine* (*TIM*) they 'solved significantly more puzzles than children playing alone on one machine' (Inkpen *et al.*, 1995). Children were also more motivated to continue playing when they had a human partner. There is no evidence that games, or any other software for that matter, can teach thinking skills on their own. However, games can be used as a resource to help teach thinking when made part of teaching and learning dialogues. The discussion of strategies and sharing of experience can capitalise on children's deep involvement with a game, helping them to understand how they can learn and develop.

Networks as a support for learning dialogues

Computers can support and provide resources for learning conversations with others in the same class – or elsewhere. Children can work with others face to face or at a distance via email or electronic conference. An example might be taking a particular topic to research together in order to develop joint multimedia resources on the web. The process of jointly constructing documents can help individuals to construct knowledge. Children's online discussion can require the same thinking skills as teachers expect when children talk face-to-face (see Chapter 2); for example, a conference might allow children the opportunity to engage one another in critical questioning, negotiation or reasoning. This is much more likely to happen if the teacher and learners are all aware that thinking together is an aim for the activity.

The claims that electronic conferencing can help children learn thinking skills relates to the specific way in which the medium supports discourse. Conferencing may support productive talk because:

- it may be possible to 'take the floor' more readily than in comparison with face to face discussion;
- the possibility of having several strands of conversation simultaneously can support a more meta-cognitive reflection on the content of the discussion;
- the written nature of the dialogue combined with asynchronicity can allow time for reflection while maintaining the intrinsic motivation of a conversation.

But for some children joining in with an electronic discussion is actually more problematic than face-to-face talk. The discussion is written and is in this way recorded, which seems to make it more important to choose words carefully. A simple lack of typing skills can be a real handicap to fluent contribution. Some prefer to reflect on what they read and may not then feel that they can re-introduce a topic as the discussion has moved on. 'Lurking' (reading without contributing) can be a useful strategy but is ultimately limited as a learning experience. The mix of skills required to become adept at conferencing is different from those required for face to face discussion. The crucial importance of shared, agreed ground rules becomes clear when inappropriate language, content or tone causes participants to become angry, to 'flame' a particular contributor or to terminate their involvement. Learning conversations are a product of careful framing of conferencing within an understanding of shared purposes and intents. Of course, highly interesting and exciting discussion can develop by chance in unstructured conference encounters. But in primary classrooms there may not be the luxury of allowing chance to dictate what learning occurs. The teacher's involvement in ensuring that conferencing is well organised allows children to be much more likely to engage one another productively. The context the teacher can provide includes the following:

- Jointly created and agreed ground rules for talk. These may deal with, for example, turn taking; vocabulary; following a line of reasoning; contributing information; challenging others.
- A shared purpose for the conferencing discussion. This should include an awareness that the quality of the discussion and how it is conducted is a learning aim for the session.
- A meaningful topic on which a range of opinions and ideas can be considered and debated.
- Ensuring that all participants have the technical and typing skills to participate equally.

Set up in this way conferences and email exchanges can provide insight and information, motivation and stimulation. The technology itself is exciting and involving, but the chance to meet the minds of interested and interesting others can be equally engaging.

Shared databases

CSILE, which stands for Computer Supported Intentional Learning Environments (Scardamalia and Bereiter, 1991), consists of a number of networked computers in a classroom where a community database is maintained. The database consists of text and graphical notes, all produced by students and accessible through database search procedures. Teachers work with CSILE in different areas of the curriculum. Students are given a question. They use the database and other resources to find information which is then recorded into the database as notes. Other students then comment on the notes and add new notes of their own. Evaluations of learning outcomes in CSILE classrooms are positive. The findings reflect the development of thinking skills, including deeper comprehension of texts and better explanations of processes. In addition the research notes that students develop a more positive self-image as learners.

ICT and creativity

Creativity is often described as a thinking skill or at least as an important aspect of thinking that can and should be fostered. In a review of the links between technology, learning and creativity, Loveless brings out some of the many ways in which ICT can support creativity (Loveless, 2002). Technology which allows children, quickly and easily, to produce high quality finished products in a range of media obviously provides opportunities for creativity. But it is also true that the provisional and infinitely correctable nature of ICT-held data encourages creativity and risk-taking. It is sometimes easier for children to be creative with a word-processor for example, where they can cut and paste, and copy and delete, than with pencil and paper where once they have committed themselves there is often no going back without the penalty of unattractive crossings out or smudgy eraser marks. But this opportunity for creativity is not enough on its own. Loveless argues that to foster creativity in the classroom, teachers need to create a social atmosphere in which children feel secure enough to play with ideas and to take risks. This atmosphere could reasonably be called one of 'collaborative creativity'.

ICT can also be used to serve as the medium for creative collaborations at a distance. Collaboration between children and artists, writers or fictional characters in 'non-residence' through email and video conferences can develop creative thinking. For example, junior children in Robin Hood School in Birmingham used video conferencing facilities to establish contact with artist Nick Eastwood, to look at his work, to ask him questions and to receive feedback from him on their own work created in response to the experience (at http://www.becta.org.uk/technology/desktopvc/telecomms/art.html). In another example, the Bristol Internet Project, children in schools in two different communities in the city collaborated with each other on making visual images over time and distance. They used digital cameras and 'paint' programs to construct images of themselves which were attached to email messages to their 'key pals' in the other school, asking questions such as 'Who am I?' Artists in each school worked with the children to interpret, respond to and manipulate the images received before sending them back with their developed ideas (Loveless, 2000).

These examples suggest some ways in which ICT can help develop creativity. Evaluations of the success of such projects are difficult. However, one of the factors that all commentators agree to be important is establishing an atmosphere of trust in which risk-taking can flourish. This is not created by technology but by the way in which children respond to each other.

The need for teaching and learning dialogues

This chapter has summarised some of the findings of recent research on ICT and thinking skills: for more information, see Wegerif (2002). One principle to emerge from this review is that using computer-based technology on its own does not produce transferable thinking skills. The success of any ICT activity crucially depends on how it is framed by teachers. Learners need to know what are the thinking skills that they are learning and these need to be explicitly modelled, drawn out and re-applied in different contexts.

Another principle to emerge is that collaborative learning improves the effectiveness of most activities. Computer mindtools such as concept maps and programming languages also all appear to be enhanced when used in pairs or groups especially when students are taught to explicitly articulate their strategies as they work together. Throughout this book, we advocate the Thinking Together approach to ICT use, a collaborative approach in which children are aware of the crucial importance of their discussion. Group work becomes meaningful as children understand how to do better together than they could do alone. They also understand that by working thoughtfully with others, they are learning how to think more clearly in situations when they must work alone.

The Thinking Together approach can be summarised in four points each of which assumes the crucial importance of teachers:

- The class undertakes explicit teaching and learning of talk skills which promote thinking.
- Computers are used both to scaffold children's use of these skills and to bridge them in curriculum areas.
- Introductions and closing plenaries are used to stress aims for talk and for thinking as well as to review progress.
- Teacher intervention in group work is used to model exploratory talk.

Computers remain one resource amongst many that support the work of teachers. Papert's idea was that computers could be used to promote thinking skills in a way that could revolutionise conventional education. However, Papert expected that interaction between the child and the software would directly promote the sort of skills that the child could then use in other situations. But the evidence suggests that computers only support the development of transferable thinking skills when they are used to provide contexts for learning dialogues.

Summary

There seems to be no evidence that children reliably learn general thinking skills just by working with computers, even if they use the programming languages and 'mindtools' that have been promoted as a way of learning to think. However, there does appear to be good evidence that some ICT activities can be used to teach general thinking skills when used as a resource for teaching and learning dialogues. Talking to others while working at the computer encourages the articulation of strategies and so increases the likelihood of learning skills that can be transferred to new situations. The teacher has a crucial role in making the thinking aims of activities explicit, modelling good thinking strategies and designing learning activities so that skills learnt in one context are applied in new contexts.

Part II

TALKING AND THINKING WITH ICT AND THE CURRICULUM

5

ICT AND CITIZENSHIP

Joining the dialogue

Computers can play an important part in the development of good citizens and good citizenship in a broad sense. We show how ICT can be used to empower children to become effective participants in the important dialogues that shape their lives and the world they live in.

Bubble Dialogue

Working in the strife-torn atmosphere of Northern Ireland in the late 1980s, Harry McMahon and Bill O'Neill, both teacher-educators at Ulster University, developed a new approach to the use of computers to support citizenship (McMahon and O'Neill, 1993). As is so often the case with new discoveries this happened almost by accident. Harry had a Macintosh computer and, one Christmas, he was given a book on creative ways to use Macintosh's simple multimedia authoring programme, HyperCard. He tried this out by making a children's story about his dog Ginny. He showed his story to his friend Bill who told him that it was too adult centred – too much just Harry's 'voice' – and it did not reflect how children saw life. Harry responded by adding thought and speech bubbles for Ginny and the other characters in the story. His idea was to pause the story at key points and ask his audience of children to fill in the bubbles.

Meanwhile, Bill's 6-year-old daughter, Orla, was also using HyperCard to make picture stories. Orla's drawings had character but Bill found her text very dull, consisting of a flat account of things that happened to her. To help her he added Harry's bubbles to her pictures. Both Bill and Harry were impressed by the results. With the bubbles Orla's characters came to life. They thought about the consequences of their actions. They took each other's point of view into account, negotiated for leadership and generally began to reflect some of the real richness of Orla's experiences and ideas.

Harry and Bill wanted to try out their thought and speech bubble idea in classrooms. Their first opportunity came with a history project about the battle of Derry in a Londonderry school. A group of five 13-year-old girls agreed to create what Harry and Bill now called a 'Bubble Dialogue'. Their focus was a modern statue on the old walls of the city: this consisted of two figures in chains, back-to-back, with their arms outstretched, one was looking over the Catholic Bogside where the girls lived while the other faced the largely Protestant walled city. To reflect the opposing sides in the Battle of Derry they called one figure the Williamite and the other the Jacobite. In a classroom situation, these academic names quickly became simplified to 'Protestant' and 'Catholic'. Harry helped by typing the girls' ideas into the programme without comment. The group rapidly created the following strange dialogue between the two statues:

JACOBITE SAYS: When I was a young boy life was hard. We hadn't got half as much as you had and we still don't. You've got a swimming pool and we've got nothing. Your toilets are twice the size of ours.

JACOBITE THINKS: Its not fair. You and your stupid swimming pool. You're no better than us.

WILLIAMITE SAYS: Our ancestors fought hard for what we've got. We shouldn't have to suffer for what happened years ago.

WILLIAMITE THINKS: The Protestants are the better race. History can prove that.

JACOBITE SAYS: We are the rightful religion because Catholic was the original religion in Ireland. The Protestant religion is only the recent thing.

WILLIAMITE SAYS: The only reason there had to be new religion was because the old one was wrong.

JACOBITE THINKS: The original religion wasn't good enough for you and your private swimming pool.

JACOBITE SAYS: It wasn't wrong; it just didn't suit you and your fancy ways.

JACOBITE THINKS: Its not fair. You and your stupid swimming pool. You're no better than us.

WILLIAMITE SAYS: Let's not go over all this all over again. Anyway, my arms are killing me.

JACOBITE THINKS: My arms are killing me too, but I'm not going to let a Protestant get the better of me.

Harry understood that the phrase 'my arms are killing me' was a joke about how the statues must feel holding their arms out all day and not an ironic reference to the civil war in Northern Ireland. However, he had no idea why these statues, representing historical figures after all, should be talking about swimming pools and toilets. The class teacher explained that the girls had recently visited a school in the Protestant area as part of an 'Education for Mutual Understanding' project. They had been struck by the resources of the other school, especially their swimming pool and the quality of their new toilet block. The Bubble Dialogue exercise had revealed that a project designed to increase mutual understanding may have served to reinforce prejudices. However, it also 'provoked' these children into trying to state the opposing viewpoints of the characters.

The teacher felt that this dialogue was a much more effective starting point for a debate about the differences between the two communities than any text she could give them because it reflected their real views. She decided to ask the girls to write a new dialogue, but this time with the statues in the Bubble Dialogue programme drawn facing each other rather than facing away from each other. She hoped that this symbolic change, with additional guidance and teaching, would help the children to consider the opposing perspectives more deeply.

Some teachers may feel that the recently introduced citizenship curriculum is an added burden in the already crowded timetable. However, it is interesting that in the context of the continuing sectarian struggles in Northern Ireland, many teachers, like Harry and Bill, feel that some version of citizenship education lies at the heart of what education is about. That is, taking a broad perspective, helping children to develop the values and skills to find peaceful solutions to real or potential conflicts might be a more important goal than raising SAT test scores. In Northern Ireland, Harry and Bill found that a simple program like Bubble Dialogue could help teachers with this challenging task. The reason for this is, they argue, that computers support communication while providing just the right amount of distance to encourage questioning and critical thought. The 'statues' in the Bubble Dialogue program could be made to say what the children were really thinking without getting them, the children, into trouble. At the same time using statues as proxies could allow them to consider and understand a different perspective from their own without, at least initially, putting their own sense of identity at risk. Teachers and learners could evaluate dialogues, contributing to discussion about what each statue might really think or say, or suggesting supplementary ideas. Through the structured use of ICT the thoughts and feelings of the children could be turned into a story which provided an object for shared reflection. This process allowed individuals to articulate and clarify their perceptions and opinions, to share them with others, creating real possibilities for change.

Harry McMahon and Bill O'Neill worked with the software HyperCard which is simple to use but only runs on Macintoshes and has been superseded by other software. Bill O'Neill died in 2001. With Harry's support we have taken the basic ideas of Bubble Dialogue and updated them to run on any platform and also accept audio input so that children do not need to type. This new version is available free to teachers and researchers from our web site. It is currently in use in citizenship lessons and teachers have found it an effective resource, allowing children to think through and share ideas.

ICT can be especially effective for supporting dialogues in citizenship. The computer can offer a range of engaging scenarios. Graphics, sound and movement provide support for visual, auditory and kinaesthetic learners. The screen, keyboard and mouse are a focus for groups constraining them to work closely together physically. We have found that the infinite 'patience' of computers allows them to stimulate extended discussions. Similarly, the absence of any judgement allows computer software to prompt talk in which feelings are revealed. A final advantage for the computer version of Bubble Dialogue over any possible paper-based version is that the task is more motivating: the characters who talk to them appear more 'real' to the children and the engagement with discussion is therefore more important.

To give one example of this, Bubble Dialogue is in use in a special school for children with emotional and behavioural difficulties. Teachers at the school believe that collaborative use of the software has great potential value. An example of the high quality of such dialogue is provided in Bubble Dialogues (in Sequences 5.1–5.3). These were created by Charline and Rory, both aged 10 years, and both excluded from their previous schools because of behavioural difficulties. They are discussing a Bubble Dialogue scenario about a personal conflict involving characters called Joe and Greg. In the story Greg was using his new skateboard in the playground when Joe, a bigger boy, grabbed it from him (see Figure 5.1(a)). The dialogue Charline and Rory constructed begins with Sequence 5.1, 'Come on', which starts with some rather violent language.

Sequence 5.1 (Bubble Dialogue) Come on

GREG SAYS: If you don't give me that back I'm going to punch your lights out.
GREG THINKS: I hate Joe...
JOE THINKS: I hate Greg.
JOE SAYS: Come on just bring it on.
GREG SAYS: I'm not scared of you, you big fat ugly baboon.
GREG THINKS: I'll have him down in no time.

In this exchange both characters 'square up' for a physical fight. However, the next set of think bubbles that Charline and Rory produced indicate that while both parties are prepared to fight over the skateboard neither really wants to.

Sequence 5.2 (Bubble Dialogue) I'm not scared

JOE THINKS: He just have to ask nicely.
JOE SAYS: I'll kick your head in you fat brat head.
GREG SAYS: Yeah come on then, I'm not scared of you if I'm a big fat brat head what does that make you, you peebrain.
GREG THINKS: I'm not scared of him all hes got to do is give me my skateboard back and apologise to me if he doesn't I'm going to break his big fat ugly bogied up nose.

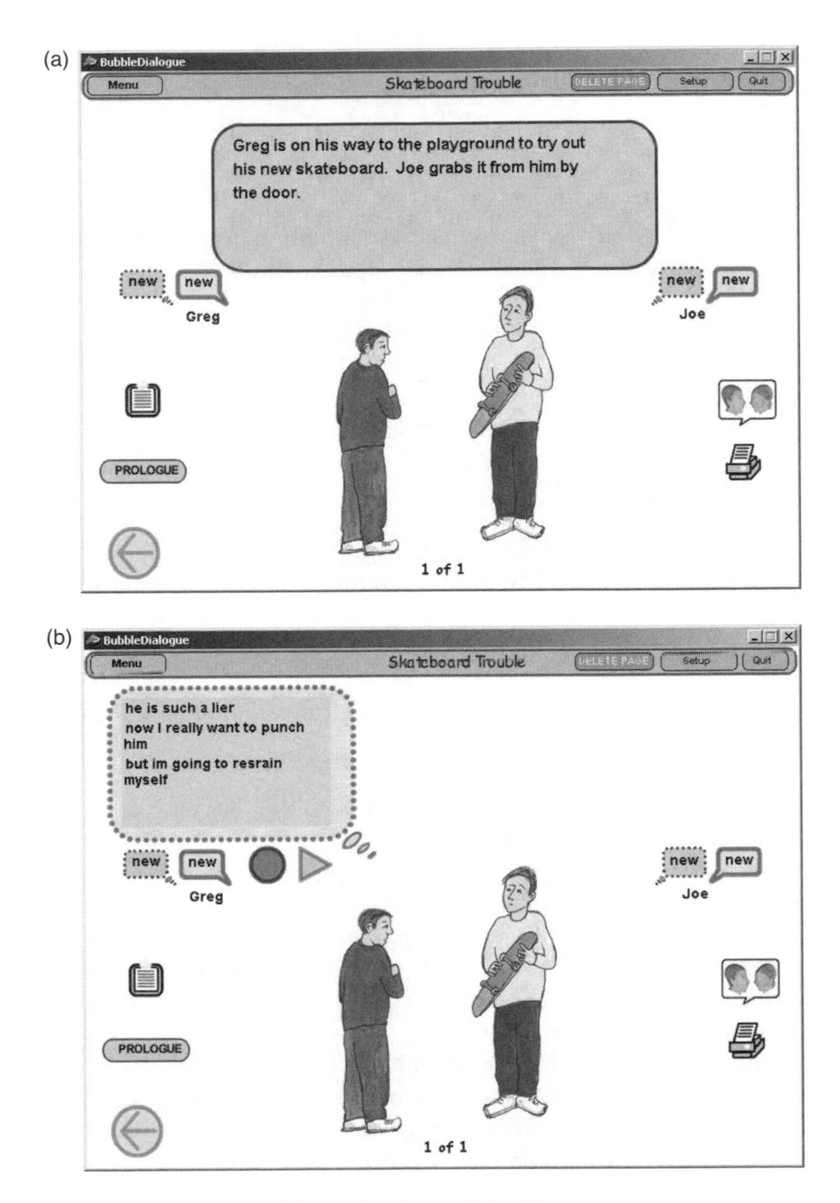

Figure 5.1 Skateboard trouble. (a) Prologue (b) self-restraint.

Charlene and Rory's story goes on to have Joe give Greg the skateboard back. When Greg insists on an apology Joe denies having taken the board and says that Greg should say sorry for threatening to punch his lights out when he was only playing. Eventually, they both manage to apologise in a guarded way and agree to be friends. Their thoughts remain angry but their words are conciliatory.

Sequence 5.3 (Bubble Dialogue) Why should I?

GREG THINKS: Why should I say sorry when he brought this on himself I don't owe him anything but...
GREG SAYS: Sorry but you shouldn't have stole my skateboard in the first place lets forget about this and be friends...please.
JOE THINKS: Yeah ok.
JOE SAYS: Why would I steal your bord when I have already got one but let's just be friends.
GREG SAYS: You cheeky rat you did steal my bored and you know it but lets forget about it and go and do something?
GREG THINKS: He is such a lier now I really want to punch him but I'm going to resrain myself.

Here the dialogue entered a new phase. Up to this point Rory and Charline had collaborated to create a 'virtual' disagreement and its resolution. They had worked well together but now an issue came up about which they really did disagree. Rory now suggested:

JOE SAYS: 'After school do you want to brick the abandoned house where the poorman lives? It'll be fun!'

Charline obviously disliked this idea and replied that her mother would not like her to do that. Throwing bricks through the windows of an empty house where a homeless person lived was apparently Rory's idea of a fun activity but not Charline's. She suggested that Greg would pretend to go along with the idea but with no intention of turning up. In doing she was also perhaps finding a way for herself to cope with similar difficult situations when she might come under peer pressure to do something that she did not want to do (Figure 5.1(b)).

The expert teachers of children with emotional and behavioural difficulties are convinced that these kinds of conversations can equip children like Charline and Rory with inner resources to draw on in real life situations. Through using the Bubble Dialogue program they rehearsed a way to talk themselves out of a fight that at first seemed inevitable. Charline has also practised a way to respond to unwelcome peer pressure to do something illegal or immoral. This was done without conflict or stress because the youngsters spoke only through proxies, the Bubble Dialogue characters Joe and Greg: it was not Charline who disagreed with the 'bricking' idea, for example, but her character 'Greg' and it was not Rory who proposed this idea, after all, but his character 'Joe'. In this example we can see how the ICT-based nature of the activity provides opportunities to support collaborative activity that print materials alone would not provide. Like other citizenship software, Bubble Dialogue provides a comic book format but one that is interactive, allowing the children to make their characters act and speak and so serve as their proxies. This is combined with easy ways for the group to record their thoughts.

What is 'citizenship'?

There are many ways of thinking about citizenship. Some people think about citizenship in terms of knowing about the practical workings of political institutions. While this aspect of citizenship is obviously important it does not feature strongly in the guidelines for Personal Health and Social Education (PHSE) and citizenship in the primary curriculum. Here the stress is more on the moral development of children and developing 'skills of enquiry, communication and responsibility' (http://www.dfes.gov.uk/citizenship/). These guidelines recognise that the roots of democracy lie in the way that people treat each other. Core values in any democracy are respect for different views and a commitment to using dialogue and reason to solve disputes. These are also the core values taught and practised in the Thinking Together approach to teaching and learning. Citizenship, understood in this way as consisting of processes and values, is not so much a separate curriculum subject as part of the way in which every subject is taught and learnt and part of the context of the life of the school. Good citizenship can be embodied in the way that groups work together, in the class ethos, in the relationship between teachers and children, and in children's engagement with the school as a community and with communities beyond the school. Citizenship, in this broad sense, is about the development of the whole person as a member of a variety of communities. The development of the whole person is understood to involve their active participation in the development of their communities.

Previous chapters have stressed cognitive gains and raised curriculum achievement gained from using computers in conjunction with Thinking Together. But teachers have also reported another type of change. This is a change in the behaviour of children and in the ethos of classrooms. For example, Deputy Head Teacher Tara Lovelock taught her Year 5 class the Talk Lessons and used the approach throughout her teaching. She describes how:

> In group work, the children began to listen to each other's ideas rather than all talking at the same time. Each member of the group felt valued, and even if they had a difference of opinion, individuals understood that the group needed to keep talking and come to a consensus of opinion before moving forward.
>
> Children also began to use the skills taught in these sessions outside the classroom, to solve disputes on the playground. Their

> attitudes to each other were more positive as they began to value each other's qualities and contributions.
>
> It is important to note that this group of children had two concentrated periods of talk lessons over two years. They became the calmest year group in the school and continued to use the skills taught in the talk lessons throughout Years 6 and 7, even though the course had finished.
>
> (Lovelock and Dawes, 2001)

Many other teachers have reported changes in the way that their children solve disputes even in the playground. Here is what one teacher had to say about the changes she observed in a Key Stage 2 class:

> They are learning a lot more collaboratively, and listening to each other rather than just hearing each other and they make sure that everyone in the group is involved. They feel more empowered... They know that it's alright if you say something, then don't necessarily want to follow that idea through. Also if they've got an idea, they know it's alright to voice it...Children...learned to talk together, and not argue or get into fights, but were able to have some quite good discussions.

The children involved in the project also had some similarly positive things to say about their experience. They recognised an improvement in the way they were able to use talk to get things done working in groups with their classmates:

> It has helped us if we are working in groups – now we've got the Rules for it as well it's made us think, 'Oh, if one person's talking we can't barge in and talk in front of them.' ...We normally take it in our turns and say 'What do you think?' instead of leaving someone out. ...(I'm not) afraid to challenge someone with their answer – (I) don't just sit there and say 'All right – *pick* that one. I don't care'. (It) makes us feel more confident if we're in a group.

These changes in group work and classroom ethos relate directly to some of the stated aims of the PHSE and Citizenship curriculum:

- to resolve differences by looking at alternatives, making decisions and explaining choices;
- to talk and write about their opinions, and explain their views, on issues that affect themselves and society;
- to recognise what they like and dislike, what is fair and unfair, and what is right and wrong;

- to share their opinions on things that matter to them and explain their views;
- to think about themselves, learn from their experiences and recognise what they are good at;
- to take part in discussions;
- to take part in a simple debate about topical issues;
- to recognise choices they can make, and recognise the difference between right and wrong;
- to agree and follow rules for their group and classroom, and understand how rules help them.

(National Curriculum for PHSE and Citizenship, KS1. The KS2 aims are similar.)

It seems that the aims and achievements of the Thinking Together approach fit very well with the citizenship curriculum. Used in conjunction with Talk Lessons, computers have a distinctive and valuable role to play. Computers can offer realistic and engaging scenarios and narratives. They can allow children to take on roles or express views through proxies. They can provide accurate and graphic information about the lives of others, present and past, and can help children to formulate and express what they think in a format open to reflection, evaluation and re-drafting. We will describe here some further ways that ICT can help create and support good citizens and good citizenship.

Kate's Choice

Chapter 2 explains how Kate's Choice (available free from the Thinking Together web site) was used to measure changes in the way that groups talked together at computers. Kate's Choice is a branching narrative providing children with moral dilemmas. Should Kate tell her parents that her friend Robert stole a box of chocolates? Depending on their decision, children are then faced with further dilemmas. Should Kate tell her friends, who are just curious and promise not to tell anyone else? Should she tell the shopkeeper who explains how her financial losses from continual theft might force her to close her community shop? If Kate refuses to tell the secret will she be accused of stealing the chocolates? What will be the consequences? In this program, eventually the secret comes out and the police are called in. To some calling the police in over the thefts of a box of chocolates seemed a little extreme but this was, in fact, the standard procedure in the schools that we worked with to pilot-test the software. Robert is then shown looking shame-faced talking to a policeman in full uniform. At this point the children are asked to reflect over their version of the whole story and decide if they are happy that Kate really did do the right thing. To help them consider this new question, they are provided with the views of all the participants in the story.

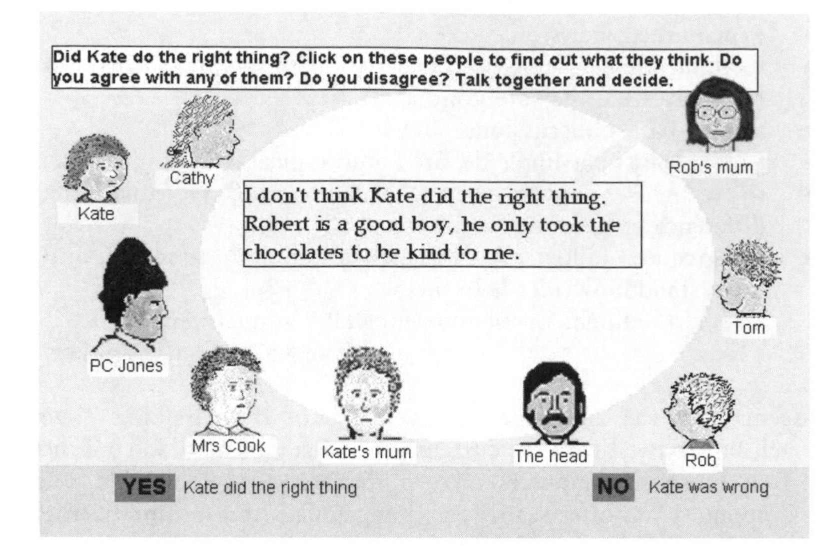

Figure 5.2 Did Kate do the right thing?

Figure 5.2 presents the screen showing the opinion of Robert's mother. Without Talk Lessons most children simply did not understand what was expected of them when asked to 'Talk Together' by the computer. However, when used in combination with the Talk Lessons, this software produced some memorable IDRF conversations. Sequence 5.4, 'Did Kate do the right thing?' illustrates the enormous potential for computer use within the citizenship curriculum. Michelle, Alan and John are 9-year-old children who had previously undertaken Talk Lessons. 'Mrs Cook' is the shop keeper.

Sequence 5.4 Did Kate do the right thing?

Computer text initiation: 'Did Kate do the right thing? Click on these people to find out what they think. Do you agree with any of them? Do you disagree? Talk together and decide'

MICHELLE: (*reading the screen text shown in Figure 5.2*)
I don't think Kate did the right thing, Robert is a good boy. He only took the chocolates to be kind to me.
ALAN: No I don't agree.
MICHELLE: I don't agree with that –
ALAN: That's just wrong.
MICHELLE: Robert's Mum should be on Mrs Cook's side really.
ALAN: Yeah. She should be more strict.

JOHN: Next round. Kate's Mother. (*Clicks on Kate's mum*)

ALAN: OK *(reads from screen)* 'Kate did the right thing to tell. She should not lie to me or hide things from me. I am her Mother.'

MICHELLE: Alright John – you go first this time.

JOHN: I think that's alright actually, because if you don't tell her, and her mother finds out she's going to get really done because she ain't told her mum.

MICHELLE: Yeah, then Kate's Mum will go round to Rob's Mum's house and say 'You did this and you did that and your son is a bad influence to my daughter.'

ALAN: 'Cos he stole

MICHELLE: But that's wrong as well. I know Kate *should* have told her Mum – and that's what she did, but if Kate didn't tell her Mum, then Rob's Mum would sort of fall out with Kate's Mum because I think Rob's Mum and Kate's Mum are friends so I think Kate's Mum is right. I agree with Kate's Mum.

ALAN: Yes. I think about Kate's Mum – and it's also good for Kate, because she'll have a really guilty conscience and she'll feel really upset inside. And she'll-

MICHELLE: And it will all start to bubble up inside her and she'll just have to tell somebody.

ALAN: And Rob, I think if he doesn't get told now what's right and what's wrong, when he gets older he's going to get into a lot more trouble than just a box of chocolates.

MICHELLE: Yes – in older life there's no second chances. He'd better start learning.

This is a short extract from this groups' talk in response to the initial challenge by the computer program: Did Kate do the right thing? The relish with which they tackle the issues is most striking. They seem to really enjoy challenging adults like Robert's mum and pointing out that she is 'just wrong'. They also enjoy the opportunity to express themselves and rehearse their own moral opinions. As well as exhibiting features of Exploratory Talk this talk fulfils several goals of the citizenship curriculum. These are Key Stage 2 children and one of the aims of the Key Stage 2 citizenship curriculum is: 'to resolve differences by looking at alternatives, making decisions and explaining choices' (The National Curriculum http://www.nc.uk.net).

This well-conducted IDRF discussion is evidence that the children have achieved this objective. It is interesting to see how the software helps them to do so. By presenting a range of different viewpoints, the software makes it easy for the children to locate themselves within a moral dialogue. One way of thinking about moral development is precisely as becoming a participant in moral dialogues. It is hard to imagine this group talking so long and so well without the 'patient and tolerant' support which the computer provides. The computer is a good listener. This software also allows the children to generate and articulate original ideas. Conversations with teachers may contain much of the teacher's viewpoint, but here the computer simply provides information and leaves the children to formulate their own opinions. But it is interesting that the computer has stimulated this discussion and framed it in such a way that it meets desired learning outcomes.

The obvious enthusiasm of the children may reflect how seldom they get an opportunity to express their own views in classroom situations. There is never enough time for everyone in whole class sessions. This small group work focussed by the computer screen provides a real opportunity for everyone's voice to be heard. An interesting feature of the talk is the way that the children are learning through practising phrases that they may have first heard elsewhere – for example, the idea of a guilty conscience 'bubbling up inside' expressed by Alan, or that 'in older life there are no second chances' expressed by Michelle. These phrases sound slightly out of place, as if the children have heard them used by their parents or in a TV drama. By having opportunities to practice moral language and think through a range of viewpoints children can develop a responsible moral voice that they really feel is their own.

Moral development and engagement in dialogues

One purpose of the citizenship curriculum is to encourage moral development; the study of moral development is a field of research in psychology. It is widely accepted in this field that moral development does not happen through being told society's rules and values, but is a gradual process through which children actively transform their understanding of morality and social convention during reflection on their own experience. That is, children's development is a product of their own meaning-making rather than passive compliance with a set of externally imposed values. This could be called a 'constructivist' view of moral development similar to Piaget's and Papert's constructivist view of cognitive development described in Chapter 4. However, it is important to focus on moral development as induction into a certain kind of dialogue.

Michelle, Alan and John are constructing moral positions, but they are doing so in response to other moral positions as a way of entering into a moral dialogue. Their moral development is evident not just through the views they affirm but through the way in which they participate in a moral dialogue. When Michelle says: 'I know Kate *should* have told her Mum, and that is what she did, but' she seeks to distinguish between blindly accepting a rule, 'always tell your parents', and doing so on the basis of reflection. It is not only that she should have told, she also had good reasons for telling. The group conclusion is that Kate telling her mum was not just the right thing to do as a general rule but in this particular case it was also in everyone's best interests. This conclusion is a co-construction between Michelle and Alan, with John supporting them. When Alan begins: 'And Rob, I think if he doesn't get told now what's right and what's wrong, when he gets older he's going to get into a lot more trouble...' he is continuing and extending Michelle's line of thought to argue that it is in Robert's long-term best interests that Kate tells his secret, because if he does not learn to consider stealing wrong he might continue and this would lead to more serious trouble later in his life. Making moral decisions on the basis of a judgement of what is in the long-term best interests of everyone concerned seems a reasonable approach. The children may be wrong about some of the facts; perhaps Robert's mum and Kate's mum are not friends, perhaps Kate will not be troubled by a guilty conscience, perhaps Robert will not get into trouble later on; but the general method of assessing the long-term impact on all concerned and seeking the outcome that is best for everyone is hard to fault.

It seems that the thoughtful approach adopted by the group is more advanced, morally speaking, than the unquestioning loyalty to family and friends which seems to lie behind Rob's mum's position. However, what rational grounds are there for this claim? Is there a firm basis for stating that Michelle and Alan's approach is morally superior to that of Rob's mum? Such moral intuitions and principles are grounded in the core values of our society. In a democratic society, there is a commitment to the value of taking decisions about controversial issues through a free, fair and open debate between all those who are affected in any way by the decision. The democratic ideal is that everyone involved in such a debate will feel able to sign up to the final decision that emerges as one that, while it might not be in their personal interests, is nonetheless in the best interests of the community of which they are a member. This ideal is not about the substance of the decisions that are being made. This will always depend on the quality of the evidence available and quality of the debate. It is an ideal about the way in which decisions are made. There is an intimate connection between this democratic ideal and the moral ideals implicit in the practice of Exploratory Talk.

The best kind of talk for taking collective moral decisions is talk in which every one gets a chance to speak, all views are listened to with respect, reasons for proposals are given, challenged and worked on in a constructive atmosphere and the final decision is one which, if possible, everyone can agree to without any feeling of coercion. Although Exploratory Talk supported by software could be seen as simply a kind of procedure for taking decisions, engaging effectively in Exploratory Talk also involves certain changes in what could be called a personal sense of identity. For example, it is crucial to Exploratory Talk that participants are able to question their own positions and to change their minds on the basis of the evidence and the reasons that they are given by other participants. In practice, moral development is hard to distinguish from becoming a full participant in Exploratory Talk. Teaching children to engage in Exploratory Talk and using this as a teaching and learning medium across the curriculum, using ICT activities when appropriate, is therefore a direct way of fostering moral development.

Research in the psychology of moral development confirms that children gain most from peer discussions where they listen to each other, build on each others ideas and co-construct together responses to moral dilemmas (Harris and Butterworth, 2002). This evidence leads one of the leading researchers in this field, Berkowitz, to argue that teachers who wish to promote moral development, should not teach morality directly but become effective facilitators of peer discussion. The evidence from the use of programmes like Bubble Dialogue and Kate's Choice suggest that it is in the support and framing of peer discussions that computers have a distinctive role in the promotion of moral development.

Use of the Internet and web

In Sequence 5.4, Kate's Choice was helpful because it allowed the group to discuss issues and take up a position in a moral dialogue. The children's moral development was not so much in the substance of their position but in the way that they engaged in the dialogue. The scenarios of Bubble Dialogue provide simulated scenarios to support development in a similar way. The Internet and the web provide opportunities to engage with real others in dialogues about real moral and social issues. Writing in the context of religious education Julian Sterne suggests that the web can be used for work on positions (Sterne, 2004). Becoming a participant in moral dialogues requires understanding the field of possible positions and locating oneself within that field. In a sense the individual learner has to appropriate the whole field in order to have a position within it. The web offers an unlimited range of positions on different issues, both local and global. There are many sites that offer child-friendly versions of such positions. One exercise that Julian Stern suggests is to take a range of web site pages, each of which express or represent a position on an issue. He suggests trying links from sites such as RE-XS (at http://re-xs.ucsm.ac.uk/ and look up the 'ethics and moral issues' section), and the Children and WorldViews Project (at http://www.cwvp.ucc.ac.uk/), or from a local authority or local newspaper. These positions can then be discussed and evaluated in much the way Michelle, Alan and John discussed the different views expressed on Kate's Choice. There are also many bulletin boards (both of the sites mentioned here have them) which allow pupils to send in their views in response to issues and see them posted up as part of an extensive dialogue on the web.

Another approach is to engage in email exchanges and links with other schools. Talking to others at a distance is very motivating and can bring real meaning to some issues. The British Council, for example, run a 'Windows on the World' project putting schools in email contact with one another. The 'i-learn' organisation runs a host of 'learning circles' connecting students across Africa, South and North America, Australia and the Middle East, and facilitating discussion and the exchange of resources relating to the different histories, cultures, governments and geographies of the learners involved. Links with schools in the developing world can bring a more personal dimension to global issues.

Supporting whole school democracy

Schools are being encouraged to exemplify in practice the democratic ideals taught in the citizenship curriculum. For example, part of this is to ensure that decision-making procedures are transparent with reasons for decisions publicly explained. The school web site has a role to play in supporting a communicative school linked to its parents and its local community. Neil Selwyn (2002) points out that the 'developing skills of participation and responsible action strand' of the citizenship curriculum has led to a concern with the pupil-voice within the school which ICT could support. He writes that 'The school council model would appear ideally suited to ICT, using e-democracy to help establish and run regular class and form council meetings and the wider school councils and working committees.'

Selwyn argues that a range of ICT-based e-democracy applications could be used, such as voting and evaluation tools, to help representatives canvas the opinions of the school. This might overcome the problems of finding times to meet and encroaching on teaching time. This is an interesting idea but, as he points out, there is as yet little good evidence to show how an ICT-based approach to school democracy works in practice.

Conclusions

The citizenship curriculum in primary schools focuses on those processes, values and skills that are the basis of democratic decision making such as listening with tolerance to the views of others, discussing alternatives and reaching agreement together on the basis of reasons rather than force. The guidelines of the curriculum are very similar to the ground rules of Exploratory Talk which form the basis of the Thinking Together approach. This is not a coincidence. Thinking Together is concerned with ensuring that groups of children can think and learn effectively. The democratic ideal is also about how a group of people can think and learn together effectively. The citizenship curriculum recognises that while democracy might ultimately be about the government of nations, it begins with how children are treated and how they are taught to treat each other.

Citizenship, overlapping with PHSE and RE, is concerned with children's moral development. Research evidence suggests that moral development is more likely to occur through conversations with peers than with teachers. A way of considering moral development can be to think of children gradually becoming drawn into effective participation in the moral and social debates around them. This is a communicative and 'dialogic' process which ICT can support and facilitate at every stage. In classrooms, teachers can harness the visually stimulating and motivating power of computers to help children learn about and discuss a range of social and ethical issues. ICT can also support communication and participation in the dialogues that are part of a whole school democracy.

Summary

Talking effectively with others implies a number of values: respect, empathy, a sense of fairness, tolerance for differences and, above all, a rejection of coercive force in favour of persuasion. A focus on dialogue, discussion and reasoning can therefore communicate the core values promoted by the citizenship curriculum. Talk can be stimulated by software which is designed to engage children in moral reasoning about ethical dilemmas. Transcript evidence reveals how software can help groups of children discuss issues that matter to them. Similar principles can be applied to the use of web sites, bulletin boards, email links and conferences to involve children in dialogues about citizenship issues with others beyond their classroom.

6

SCIENCE, TALK AND ICT

While learning through discussion is obviously of value in subjects such as citizenship, some might see problems in applying this approach to subjects such as science. This chapter describes how the Thinking Together approach can be used in conjunction with computer-based activities in a way that takes account of the specific requirements of the science curriculum.

Sara and the 'Talking Bug'

Teacher Sara Adjani was enthusiastic about the Thinking Together approach in general but was concerned about applying this to teaching science. The ground rules of Exploratory Talk, she pointed out, are all very well for discussing moral dilemmas where everyone may have a different view, but in science some conceptions are well established; children should be provided with access to our current understanding of how the world works. She had tried group work in science sessions and found that groups could talk together to share misconceptions. She described how a group working with a CD-ROM about animals attempted to answer the question, 'What do frogs eat?' At the end of the session, the children insisted that frogs eat grass. The group had discussed the question and been persuaded by the argument of Kieran who said that he kept a frog as a pet at home and that his frog definitely ate grass. Sara's point was that it was her job as a teacher to ensure that the children understood that frogs eat insects, not grass. She thought that asking the children to discuss this factual point was almost bound to create problems because it offered an opportunity for persuasive children to spread their misunderstandings.

This is a good point. Group discussion cannot always lead to an understanding of current conceptions of science 'facts'. But Sara felt that discussion could help children to share their thoughts, and to understand and remember ideas. Providing the information that frogs eat flies might not mean very much unless the children could connect this with information about how the frog's physical structure is adapted to its habitat.

Children require opportunities to reflect on such concepts in order to understand them. It seems likely that children can better understand the principles of science when the 'facts' provide answers to questions they have asked as individuals, or groups.

Sara's class of 9- and 10-year olds were considering how sound is transmitted differently through a range of materials. Software simulations allow learners to select a material and measure how much sound is transmitted in a 'virtual test' situation. Such simulations can provide a strong focus for group work and generate a useful context for considering ideas about science through collaborative talk.

Children generally enjoy using computer programs to click buttons and see things move or flash or make noises. However, they seldom 'step back' from the screen to discuss what they see and find out through using the software. The chance to learn and understand may be lost if children do not reflect on what is happening and what the simulation is telling them. One of the most valuable aspects of learning science is that by working through enquiry children can acquire a logical, analytical and creative way of thinking. How could the computer simulation of measuring sound insulation help children to work in this way?

Sara decided that groups of children should first plan a 'fair test' which involved changing one variable at a time. They were asked to predict which material would provide the best insulation against sound, and why. In this way their own ideas about the problem and their own prediction would help them to make meaning from the computer's 'answer'. The discussion of a fair test and a prediction would provide a strong context in which the virtual experiment could be conducted. Groups were asked to observe carefully what actually happened, recording measurements and taking notes, and try to explain what they found out and why their prediction was right or wrong. The final step in this process was communicating their question, method and results to others. This process was summarised as:

1 Ask a question;
2 Plan a test;
3 Predict the outcome, giving a reason;
4 Run the test;
5 Observe what happens;
6 Explain the outcome in light of your prediction;
7 Communicate what you did and what you found.

Rather than providing a paper-based worksheet to guide the children through this process, we devised a programme that would run in conjunction with an existing computer simulation. This programme would prompt the children to talk together when decisions were necessary, when results required analysis, and so on. It was designed to work together with

Figure 6.1 Science Explorer Sound Lab.
Source: Science Explorer II by Granada Learning.

Figure 6.2 Talking Bug at rest.

software chosen by Sara: Granada's popular 'Science Explorer' software which includes a simulation of testing materials for sound insulation properties (Figure 6.1).

The additional programme was called the 'Talking Bug' because its role was to 'Bug' or bother learners into talking together. It communicated with the children using recorded audio messages and text messages. It was designed to look like a ladybird so that the name 'Talking Bug' was doubly appropriate.

When not active the Talking Bug sat quietly at a corner of the screen (Figure 6.2). In her introduction to the lesson Sara reminded children of their previous work on sound, set out the science aims of the lesson and emphasised the importance of using the shared ground rules for talk that had been established in earlier lessons. The children worked in groups of three. The Bug asked children to 'Click on me when you are ready'. If they forgot to follow the instructions the Bug was programmed to start twitching (flexing its wings!) and to repeat 'Click on me when you are ready' in an insistent way. Despite its irritating nature, or perhaps because of it, the Talking Bug prompted the children who used it to talk together as they worked through their investigation. Video evidence indicates that they were able to think together about their conceptions of which materials were good sound insulators. The points at which the Bug demanded attention and reminded the children to talk together were:

Opening screen: Identify variables and plan a fair test.
Before running simulation: Make predictions, giving reasons.
After running simulation: Interpret and explain findings. Check prediction against findings and decide why the prediction was right or wrong.
Using and applying findings: Decide on a fair test to apply knowledge about sound insulation in a new context.

Sara used the Talking Bug with Science Explorer in her school's computer suite. The children in her class worked at the computers in mixed ability groups of three. A group chosen by Sara as representative of the class, Sandra, Brad and Kylie, was video recorded. Sequence 6.1, 'Sound vibrations', begins with an introduction and questions from the Bug and illustrates how a computer prompt can stimulate discussion.

Sequence 6.1 Sound vibrations

TALKING BUG: In this lab you can test how well four different materials block out sound. Which material do you predict will be the best at blocking out a high-pitched sound, like a whistle? Talk together to decide and say your reasons why before you click on a button.
SANDRA: Um. Can you hear sound through wood? (*Points to wood on list.*)
BRAD: I think – What?
SANDRA: Can you hear sound through wood?
BRAD: I imagine you can, but I think that –
KYLIE: How about glass? (*Points to glass on list.*)
BRAD: No – not glass, because of the vibrations. (*He gestures to indicate vibrations.*)
SANDRA: From cloth you can.
KYLIE: Yeah, but they haven't got cloth here.
BRAD: – vibrations – metal because it can't vibrate and and it's really strong.
KYLIE: (*To Sandra*) It *is* strong isn't it. OK. Metal. (*Sandra nods.*)
SANDRA: OK. Here.
BRAD: What?

SANDRA: If you hear sound with the metal –
KYLIE: Well, you can't really 'cos if you like had metal walls, yeah, you wouldn't be able to hear anything around – brick wall-
SANDRA: (Clicks mouse on the 'METAL' button)
TALKING BUG: Thank you. Do you think this will be different for low-pitched sound?

The Talking Bug interface (Figure 6.3) is typical of a tutorial software and necessitates an IRF (initiation, response, feedback) interaction between the programme and the children. However, here the Bug, in conjunction with their previous lessons establishing ground rules for talking together around computers, leads this group of children to discuss how materials block out sound and to make an explicit prediction based upon their shared experience. The I*D*RF – Initiation, *Discussion*, Response, Follow-up – structure that we introduced in Chapter 1 is clearly illustrated. The Talking Bug programme initiates (I), the children then discuss (*D*) and make a joint response (R – a mouse click by Sandra) with a final follow-up (F) by the Talking Bug acknowledging their input and asking a new question. A further, more significant, follow-up comes later on when the Bug reminds the group of this prediction and asks them to try to explain why their investigation has shown it to be wrong.

The transcript example has some features of Exploratory Talk; it is inclusive and reasoned, information is shared, and joint agreement is

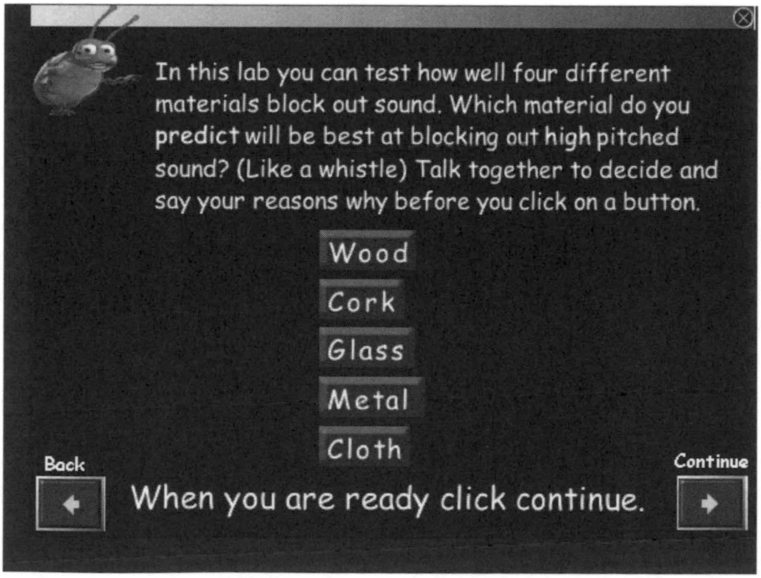

Figure 6.3 Talking Bug prompt.

sought. Brad's suggestion of 'metal' as a good sound insulator is considered by the others and accepted. Once they have tested the materials and discover that this is not the right answer they continue to question one another in a brave attempt to understand the problem they encounter, even when all seem to have run out of new ideas.

Sara's aim was to use the computer to help the children develop their conception of what materials are good sound insulators, and why. There is some evidence of achievement in this in the first half of the transcript where Brad recalls and introduces the term 'vibration' and explains what he thinks this means. He then suggests that metal, which he describes as 'strong', will not vibrate. This is inaccurate, but completely understandable in the light of the children's recent experience which was to observe and touch the resonating stretched strings of a violin. The instrument was used by the teacher to make vibration visible (therefore, more real and understandable) as well as audible. The children have formed the concept that the physical movement of the thin string, vibration, is 'why' there is sound. Brad thinks of metal as strong (i.e. rigid) and cannot envisage the visible motion which he thinks must take place in order for sound to be carried. Ironically, violin strings are made of metal. The transmission of sound in this case is through the air.

Sara's worry that the children would share misconceptions is realised. They believe that thin, flexible materials are necessary for vibration and that 'strong' (hard, rigid) materials will not vibrate therefore make good insulators. The children have no conception of how density affects sound transmission. However, the fact that this learning conversation took place helped the children to express ideas which could later be discussed in the larger whole class plenary. In addition, if we consider science as enquiry, we can see here an example of ICT supporting children as they ask questions and design a fair test. Science is not about knowing the right answer at the prediction stage!

After prompting the children to make a prediction the Talking Bug guides them through designing an investigation to test this. They learn that cork is the best insulator for high-pitched sound. The Talking Bug returns (she reminds them to click on her by twitching her wings) and asks them which material was best. When they select cork the Bug asked them to explain why their initial prediction was wrong. As they grapple with this question Sara, who had been circling the class working with different groups, joined them. She was able to build on the idea of vibrations offered by Brad and of the thickness of the material offered by Sandra to explain about the importance of density and compactness. Metal may be 'strong' but because it is very compact it transmits sound through vibration whereas cork, which is much less compact, does not. The children appear to accept this new idea. In the closing plenary, Sara, having talked to all the children as they were working in their groups, knew what misconceptions might be held and took care to reinforce the point about density.

The prompts from the Talking Bug stimulated these children to think about the science problem together. Their initial conceptions, although incorrect, give Sara something to build on in offering a scientific explanation for their experimental findings. Sara felt that the children were receptive to her offer of information because this helped them to solve an otherwise intractable problem. The question 'why isn't metal the best sound insulator?' was generated by the children themselves; they were very interested to find out the answer. Sara would go on to organise further practical activity to ensure that the children's learning experience at the computer was consolidated.

The story of Sara and how the Talking Bug motivated Brad, Kylie and Sandra illustrates how computers can be used to support teaching and learning in science. The Talking Bug is not generally available but the important point is how the task is set up and prepared by the teacher – the same effects can be achieved without specialised software. This episode was a small part of the Nuffield funded Thinking Together project in which we worked with Year 5 class teachers to enhance their science and maths teaching over one year. The sound insulation lesson was one of many computer-based activities most of which used widely available software. The common thread was that all of the activities encouraged I*D*RF exchanges of the kind described here, and that the children understood the nature and purpose of using joint ground rules to talk together. This approach was found to stimulate Exploratory Talk in contexts that supported the teacher's specific learning intentions for science.

Why talk helps learning in science

Children spontaneously create their own ideas about the way things work. This is evident, for example, in the example given here where a group of children all agreed that metal would not transmit sound because it is 'strong'. Teaching science concerns ensuring that children know that observations and ideas are subject to enquiry. That is, children's 'why?' questions are focused into queries which can be speculated about and investigated to generate answers and further questions. Teachers work with children's spontaneous ideas both to challenge them, in order to engage children in a scientific way of testing and constructing knowledge, and also to build on them, restructuring and clarifying initially fuzzy ideas.

The understanding of science concepts is tied up in words, with which we define, explain, build models and employ metaphor to convey our current thinking about the world around us. The science that children 'know', or think that they know, and the language with which they communicate this are inextricably linked. When we, as teachers, ask them to explain their ideas about the world, what they think is created and presented for us to hear in words.

The first and best way to find out what children think is to encourage them to talk. Sometimes the act of putting thoughts into words helps the children to identify what it is that they do think. Making their understanding public also makes ideas accountable to reason and to evidence and so opens ideas up to revision and development. We considered the slightly different problems of misconceptions, partial understandings and problems caused by vocabulary.

An example of a child's **misconception** from the project schools is:

TEACHER: How are shadows formed?
CHILD: The light is so bright that your body reflects it back and makes the shadow.

There are whole web pages listing children's misconceptions in different areas of science. Some of these are very poetic such as that wind is caused by the trees waving their branches or that stones fall downwards because they want to return to the earth. Such misconceptions are generated by observation and imagination. The child constructs an explanation to account for or describe their personal experience. To address these different understandings and misunderstandings children need to be given the opportunity to make their ideas public, that is, to participate in extended stretches of dialogue during which concepts are shared and vocabulary put to use to create meaning. A whole class context may not present enough opportunity for everyone to engage in such extended talk.

Children also exhibit **partial understandings**, for example:

TEACHER: Why will a sponge float?
CHILD: Light things that are full of air float.

Partial understandings are again generated by observation and experience. The child's concept may account for some or even most situations but may not be entirely accurate. Further opportunity to investigate questions and to share understanding can help children to develop their thinking. For example, groups might discuss the question: what does air do to things to make them float?

Further problems arise in science because of **alternative word meanings**:

TEACHER: Can you say what you mean by force?
CHILD: Force is strong.

The child's conception of the range of meanings of a word may be limited or even confused. Individual understandings of word meanings are most often generated by social interaction. New uses of everyday words may be difficult for learners to accommodate. This type of misunderstanding indicates why it is necessary that children learn scientific vocabulary – a never-ending task best undertaken a little bit at a time! Without the 'label' to put to the concept, thinking alone or with others will be less precise, or further misunderstandings will arise. One reason for difficulties is that words like 'condensation' and 'evaporation' when first encountered may be so rarely heard that they are difficult to retain and recall. Conversely, films and songs which make phrases like 'flux capacitor' familiar may help teachers explain some aspects of electricity. Words or phrases may be misused colloquially, for example 'the greenhouse effect' is commonly reported as a modern phenomenon threatening the planet with global warming; however, life on earth would not have arisen without it. The problem is due to enhanced greenhouse effect. A related difficulty is that of learning new uses for familiar words. For example, 'force' to a child may be synonymous with aggression: 'dark' may be a colour tone: 'north pole' may be where there are polar bears. This type of misunderstanding can be successfully addressed by encouraging children to engage in dialogues in which they have the opportunity, in a supported way, to practice using new words, or words already known, in appropriately scientific ways.

Small group work at the computer can provide chances for everyone to practice scientific vocabulary while explaining their views. However, group work in science can create problems. Learners are not always good teachers, and may not understand the need to provide the smaller steps required to help someone else develop their thinking. They may not know how to provide the sensitive intervention that is necessary for true scaffolding. They are more likely simply to provide the solution to a problem rather than break the puzzle down into manageable bits to assist others. As Sara pointed out, in groups where all learners are new to understanding a topic, group work can be a dangerous strategy: first, because talk can be difficult and opportunities to practice new words or ways of using words may not arise; and second, because group work can lead to misconceptions becoming accepted as facts.

Teacher intervention and the guided use of computers as a focus for group Exploratory Talk can help to overcome both of these difficulties. As the Talking Bug example indicates, educational software can help to break down complex science problems and procedures. The software allows computers, as partners in learning conversations, to switch modes from prompting children to talk on the one hand, to offering them resources for their discussion on the other. These range from key words to simulations to whole encyclopaedias and the myriad resources of the Internet.

Further examples of Thinking Together in science with ICT

Software which can be used successfully for teaching and learning science includes concept cartoons, sorting programmes and concept mapping software. These were used to break down learning into achievable steps, each step accompanied by chances to reflect aloud, to discuss ideas and share new vocabulary.

Concept Cartoons

Naylor and Naylor (2000) have shown that the Thinking Together approach works well in conjunction with 'Concept Cartoons' (Figure 6.4) in which children suggest alternative ideas about a puzzle with a science theme. For example, how do batteries work? Is it because they contain electricity which comes out of each end along the wires and meets in the bulb in the middle? Or because they make a spark which lights the bulb? The group discuss these and their own ideas to reach a joint, reasoned decision about what they think. This may or may not be the 'right' answer, but the talk allows the teacher to discern and address their children's misconceptions. It is then possible to address these with specifically-focused further activities.

Concept Cartoons are an excellent focus for small group discussion allowing the voices of the children in the class to be put in the thought bubbles of the characters in the cartoon. An effective lesson with Concept Cartoons involves thinking about the phases of the moon. For the teacher, explaining the reasons for the phases of the moon can be quite difficult.

Figure 6.4 Snowman Concept Cartoon.

Interactive simulations freely available on the Internet (see e.g. the NASA education site http://kids.msfc.nasa.gov/Earth/Moon/) show the way that the sun's light is reflected to us from the moon in different stages of the moon's orbit around the earth. The NASA simulation can be displayed on an interactive whiteboard or using a data-projector and a screen. This is much more effective when used as a plenary after working in groups with the relevant Concept Cartoon that is also offered free on the Virtual Teacher Centre (http://www.bgfl.org/bgfl/activities/intranet/ks2/science/what_shape_the_moon/index.htm). The Concept Cartoon offers a framework for whole class and small group discussion which sensitises children to the science issues before the experimental observations offered by the simulation. It is through talking and thinking together about issues in this way that children can construct personal conceptions of how the moon changes shape that are compatible with those generated by the scientific community.

Sorting

Software such as Flexitree is widely used to support sorting activities in science. The value of sorting activities lies in offering children opportunities to think carefully about the ways things relate to one another. That is, when children can identify key features of the objects or creatures they are sorting, they can go on to make important decision about the profound ways they are similar or different. In this way useful categorisation and classification becomes possible. A focus on shared ground rules for talking about these things ensures that the issues are deeply considered. Video recordings of children in Thinking Together classes reveal them conducting intense and fascinating discussions about whether dolphins are or are not fish: or whether pizzas should or should not go in the 'healthy food' category!

The sorting software that the children were using,[1] like others of this type, provides a drag-and-drop interface which allows them to put objects into categories. For example, what sorts of foods are high in protein, carbohydrate or fat? Or, given a tomato, a carrot and an apple, which is the odd one out, and why? Such comparison and categorisation help children to explore concepts, decide on and identify relevant similarities and differences, and create sorting systems and categories of their own.

Concept mapping

There is research evidence that using concept mapping can serve as an excellent resource for discussion in small groups (Roth and Roychoudhury, 1994). Electronic concept mapping software provides a medium for eliciting, recording, ordering thoughts in a way that is transient and open to revision, or which can be easily retained. In addition the medium itself is motivating and produces legible and attractive copy to share with the larger class. Using concept mapping as a group is much more effective for learning in science than using it for individuals working alone. Using eMindMaps with children aged 9, the Thinking Together team found that the decisions taken in order to produce a joint concept map encouraged productive group discussion of scientific ideas and the use of scientific vocabulary (Fernandez, 2001).

Sequence 6.2, 'Classifying fruit', is an example of discussion supported by Concept Mapping software. Here Samra, Angela and Darren (aged 9) have created several branches for different kinds of fruit in their concept map of healthy food. We join the group at the point where Darren has suggested the creation of a sub-branch after 'apple'. Darren suggests that this branch is labelled 'juicy'.

Sequence 6.2 Classifying fruit

SAMRA: No – do *ripe*. We can. We can actually do a sub-branch there and do ripe as well.
ANGELA: What did you say Samra?
SAMRA: Cause you know, somebody might find a green pear but is not ripe and they go ahead and eat it and be aching from a bellyache. So if we do ripe there yeah as another sub-branch it won't be a doubt.
DARREN: What do we put? What do we need? Ripe, ripe, ripe...

Samra is able to modify Darren's suggestion because she knows that there is a more scientific term than 'juicy' to describe the same phenomenon. Having thought about this, she then realised that this property did not just apply to apples but to a range of fruits. Her suggestion that the group creates a sub-branch coming after each fruit and not just after apple allows the group to improve their concept map – and develop their thinking. Here is a group using to good effect the productive mixture of Exploratory Talk and motivating software to develop a scientific classification and practise their scientific vocabulary.

Conclusion

ICT offers primary science teachers invaluable support when used to both frame and resource small group work. Children approach school science with an everyday understanding of how things work, which is sometimes based on little evidence and on much imagination. Without wishing to undervalue this – imagination should definitely be fostered – school science must address the child's entitlement to learn what generations of people have found out about the way the world works. Teaching and learning involves organising an approach based on science as enquiry, that is, science as a way of thinking in which what is 'known' is always open to question. Science as enquiry involves encouraging children to find ways to verify or establish a joint understanding, based on creating the conditions where what happens can be observed, or can be clearly visualised, noticed or recorded. School science positions children as newcomers in the community of practice of those enquiring about the world around us. As newcomers, children can be invited to describe their spontaneous conceptions about various phenomena, for example, how the seasons occur, or why things float or sink. Their subsequent development of scientific concepts can be undertaken through structured activity and mediated through oral language. Children must move forward simultaneously in their use of specialised vocabulary and ways of thinking, and in their understanding of current scientific explanations, models and ideas. New ways of using language are learned only by using them – this means that children need lots of opportunities to talk in science lessons.

Children can use jointly agreed strategies to help them to find out what their peers think, and why. They may then come to understand that this has great value for the achievement of their group which can do better in collaboration than each of them might do alone: and for themselves, as they engage in stretches of discourse in which their peers provide focused supportive assistance. Children who use the talk rules can scaffold one another's learning, not by chance, but by intent.

The benefits of Exploratory Talk around the computer for group members in science are that they are enabled to grapple with concepts and generate new 'why?' questions when they reach the limits of their understanding. The computer offers resources for science learning, relevant contexts, models, chances to try things and repeat the trial, ways to record and retrieve results, and ways to present and communicate findings. ICT can reinforce children's understanding of science as enquiry, and can lead them through the process of investigation in a way that can help them to begin to assimilate this way of approaching problems. By providing contexts where the child can ask, 'What happens if I do this – does it always happen – why? – what difference does this change make?' and so on, the computer offers much more than a superficially engaging game. By providing children with appropriate activities and talk partners engaged in pursuing thoughts with the same shared focus, teachers can take the element of chance out of what might be learnt at the computer and be assured that they have organised an enriching learning experience.

Summary

Learning science requires that children learn a new language and a new way of using language. Children's initial conceptions need to be exposed in order to be either developed or challenged. One of the most important ideas taught in science is that every conception should be subject to question and to a process of systematic shared enquiry. Children require guided opportunities to talk in order to learn science. The combination of Talk Lessons and the appropriate software can prompt questioning, provide support for structuring scientific enquiry and offer resources for experiment and exploration that allow children to develop their own ideas in a way that converges with accepted scientific concepts.

7

MATHS, TALK AND ICT

Maths software has the potential to be a focus for creative thinking and problem-solving. But much depends on how the software is used. The ideal is that children should learn to develop strategies and understand problems for themselves. This chapter shows how using maths software to help develop this sort of understanding is effective when children work together in groups and when they have been prepared by Talk Lessons to ask questions, challenge claims and offer reasons.

In Chapter 2, we described children working with co-ordinates software to locate a 'hidden elephant' in the grid-map of New York city. The children treated the software as a game in which each tried to win at the expense of their partner. As a result they learnt nothing about co-ordinates. Several years later we were able to observe children using similar co-ordinates software as part of The Nuffield funded Thinking Together project. This time the children were in a class that had worked through the Talk Lessons and the interaction between the children at the computer was quite different. A typical group of three children were recorded discussing and agreeing pairs of co-ordinates before one of them typed this into the keyboard. They gave reasons for their ideas and questioned each other, and as a result they developed their understanding of co-ordinates. Our observations of children working around co-ordinates software showed that the most important factor for achieving quality discussion is how children are prepared for working together.

The Nuffield funded Thinking Together project enabled us to see if this applied to other maths concepts. Six classes of 9-year-old children undertook the Talk Lessons designed to promote the use of Exploratory Talk before working in groups at computers, using software provided free to schools as part of the National Numeracy Strategy. Other software provided a simple co-ordinates activity, a magic-squares activity and sorting activities using numbers and shapes.

The impact of the Thinking Together programme with ICT in maths was evaluated using the official (optional) SATs questions for that year. The six target classes were matched with six control classes in similar schools who addressed the same areas of the curriculum but without Talk Lessons. The same set of questions was provided for both sets of classes at the beginning and again at the end of the school year. Children achieved low scores on the initial test which covered areas of maths that had not yet been taught. At the end of the year all children did much better. However, target classes improved noticeably more than the control classes. Statistical analysis showed that the impact of our Thinking Together approach was equivalent to moving a class from 50th position in a league table of 100 schools into the top 30 (Higgins, 2003).

This highly significant result demonstrates that the Thinking Together approach combined with ICT use can contribute to raising achievement for children. This finding shows that the approach works but how does it work so well? Can we specify how children learnt more maths by talking together while working on maths software? This question, is crucial to advice for teachers on how best to use ICT in classrooms. To answer this question, we need to look in detail at what happened in the target classrooms.

Function machine

Function Machine was given to English schools as part of the National Numeracy Strategy pack. It is a simple piece of software through which children input a number and this is transformed into an output number by a hidden function. The children have to find the hidden function by trying different input numbers and looking for a pattern.

An example is found in the classroom work of a newly qualified teacher called Jan Brown using Function Machine with children aged 8 to 9 years in a computer suite. Jan used her introduction to the lesson for three purposes:

- To refer back to previous maths lessons in order to emphasise the maths focus of the lesson on the properties of numbers.
- To remind her class of their shared ground rules for talk. She did this by asking the children to re-state key rules while she wrote them out on the whiteboard.
- To explain how the software worked and describe the activity.

In her conversation with the whole class and with individual children Jan was modelling Exploratory Talk. The school did not have an interactive whiteboard or a data-projector so the class were asked to gather close to one machine. Jan explained the working of a function machine (Figure 7.1) and then showed an example, first asking the class to suggest a number. Sequence 7.1, 'Everyone agree?', is an extract from the lesson introduction in which Jan's dialogue with the class establishes and models a way for the children to work effectively together.

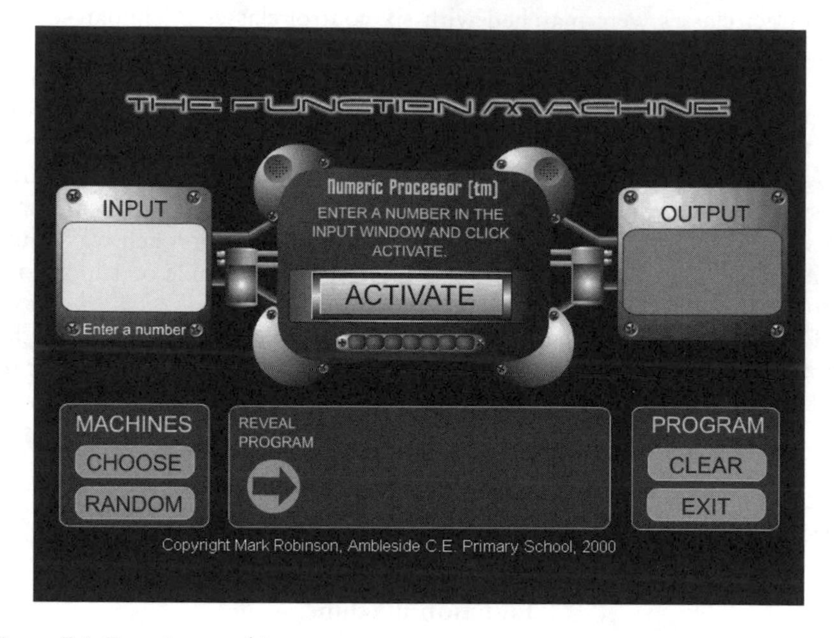

Figure 7.1 Function machine.

Sequence 7.1 Everyone agree?

TEACHER: OK. I'm going to put a number in –

LLOYD: One thousand.

TEACHER: OK. Lloyd immediately said one thousand – is that a good number to put in?

CHILD: No.

TEACHER: You are shaking your head – why do you think it is not? Shall we come back to you? You've got an idea but you can't explain it? OK. Lloyd had one thousand. Anybody think yes or no to that idea? Declan.

DECLAN: Start off with an easier number.

TEACHER: Start off with an easier number. By an easier number what kind of number do you mean?

DECLAN: Um. Something like – lower – five.

TEACHER: Fine. A smaller number – a lower number – yes. Lloyd can you see that point of view?

LLOYD: Yeah.

TEACHER: If we put in a thousand we could end up with a huge number. If we put in five do you think it will be easier to work out what the machine has done?

CLASS: Yeah.

TEACHER: Everyone agree?

CLASS: Yeah.
TEACHER: OK. I'm going to type in five...

Jan asks for reasons with 'why' questions, gives reasons for her own decisions, challenges in a respectful way, asks members of the group for their views, makes sure alternatives are discussed and tries to get all to reach an unforced agreement with her before proceeding to input anything into the computer. That is, in this short sequence she manages to model most of the ground rules for Exploratory Talk. In this way, she clearly establishes this maths activity as one in which guessing and getting the right answer is not as important as discussing ideas and working out strategies.

Jan then asked the children to work at the computers in their usual talk groups of three. On this occasion there were two groups each with a member who was absent. Jan asked these two pairs to join up into a group of four. This group was video recorded. In Sequence 7.2, 'Half the number', the group have successfully solved several problems with the Function Machine. As we join the group they have typed in the number 6. This was processed by the Function Machine giving the answer 3. The group then typed in the number 4 which generated the answer 2.

Sequence 7.2 Half the number

KAYLEIGH: So what do you think the – ?
RUBY: Take away.
KAYLEIGH: No, I think half.
THOMAS: I think you have to add on two more.
KAYLEIGH: No because – what I think – I think like Ruby, it's half the number because we had six and it ended up three. Now we had four and it ended up in two.
KAYLEIGH: No. We did it (inaudible) before, didn't we? So what do you think the – ?
RUBY: Take away.
KAYLEIGH: No, I think half.
THOMAS: I think you have to add on two more.
KAYLEIGH: No because – what I think – I think like Ruby, it's half the number because we had six and it ended up three. Now we had four and it ended up in two. Do you think half the number or subtracting? Do you want to check – shall I press reveal?
MICHAELA: (inaudible)
THOMAS: No. I think it's what Michaela said...
RUBY: What did you say?
MICHAELA: I said we tried four and it came out – I think it's half.
RUBY: Michaela said the same.
KAYLEIGH: OK. So do you want to choose a different number – try once more? Let's see if we put in an odd number and see what happens.

Thomas, who has a Statement of Special Need in Education to help address his learning difficulties, seems to be struggling a little. His confusing idea that the hidden function is to add 2 is not rejected outright, but challenged by Kayleigh who gives clear reasons for her view that the function is to halve the original number. Thomas listens but does not appear to agree and so Kayleigh suggests a very sensible test of her hypothesis, trying an odd number.

In this sequence it is possible to see how following the ground rules for talk helps the children to support each other's learning about numbers. The child with better understanding is encouraged to articulate the underlying pattern clearly and give reasons for her view. Everyone is drawn in to the discussion and significant distinctions, such as the difference between take-away and halving, are exposed.

In the plenary session Jan asked the class to evaluate their work in terms of mathematical understanding, and the quality of their talk together. She asked all the groups if they had found any problems working together and if so how they had resolved them. She also asked them about the strategies that they had found useful. She praised the idea from Kayleigh of testing to see if the function was 'divide by two' by inputting an odd number.

Research suggests that many misunderstandings in maths originate in the difference between the meanings that children ascribe to key words in maths compared to the meaning that teachers intend (Raiker, 2002). It is possible that the conflict between Ruby and Kayleigh is not so much a difference in the way that they understand the problem as in the way that they are using words. Ruby seems to think that the phrase 'taking away' can include halving while Kayleigh is clear that it cannot. Kayleigh understands 'taking away' in the more expert sense of 'subtraction' and 'halving' in the more expert sense of 'division by two'. While taking away and halving seem very similar to the mathematical novice the expert knows that subtraction and division are completely different functions. As in science it is only when the children talk together in this way that the teacher has a chance of eliciting and addressing their misconceptions. But as in science, novices need the opportunity of small group work to practice using their maths vocabulary. The ground rules for talk, with their emphasis on challenging and giving reasons, help them to question and adjust the way that they are using technical words.

Sorting

There is much software that can be used to sort data into categories. In the Nuffield Thinking Together project we used software developed for undergraduates at the Open University which allows students to generate their own categories and then sort data into YES and NO boxes. The strength of this software, called 'the Elicitation Engine', is that once students have generated their own categories to describe an area the software itself has built-in challenges to confront the students' thinking. It asks them to suggest similarities between things that they always put in different boxes. It asks for the differences between things that they always put in the same boxes. This has proved an excellent stimulus for reflection in areas as diverse as Art history and educational theory. The software was modified to make the interface easier to use for primary children. In one activity children were asked to think up categories for sorting shapes and in another to think up categories for sorting numbers. Commercially available software such as Flexitree could equally well have been used for these activities.

Sequence 7.3, 'Why do you think that?' is taken from a sorting numbers lesson with Year 5 children. As we join them the children are sorting a set of numbers according to whether or not they are multiples of 4, a category that they have just decided on for themselves.

Sequence 7.3 Why do you think that?

GURJIT: Is nine (a multiple of four)?	
SAM: No.	
MEHNAZ: No.	
GURJIT: Why do you think that?	
SAM: Um –	
SAM AND MEHNAZ: Because –	
SAM: Because it goes four, eight then twelve so it misses nine out.	
MEHNAZ: 'Cos if you do four times five it isn't –	
GURJIT: And – and only – and only the even numbers end in zero, two, four, six, eight.	
SAM: Yeah. And four is even. Eight yes –	*Gurjit drops 9 in the 'no' box and then 8 in the 'yes' box*
GURJIT AND MEHNAZ: Yes.	
SAM: Four, eight – twenty-five?	
MEHNAZ: No.	
SAM: It would be four – four, eight,	
MEHNAZ: No, no, no there's no twenty-five – no.	
SAM: No, no, no, no.	
GURJIT: It would be twenty if it was in there.	
SAM: Yeah, twenty-four!	*Gurjit puts 25 in the 'no' box*
GURJIT: Twelve is one?	
MEHNAZ: Yes.	*Gurjit puts 12 in the 'yes' box*
SAM: Yes – four, eight, twelve – three times four. Five?	
MEHNAZ AND GURJIT: No.	*Gurjit puts it in the 'no' box*

SAM: Hundred?
MEHNAZ: I don't think so. *Pause*
SAM: Yes it is – isn't it?
GURJIT: Yes it is innit, because all the times tables – the answers in the four times tables are even –innit!
SAM: That's right, yeah! Sure?
GURJIT: Are you confused? *To Mehnaz*
MEHNAZ: Yes – a little bit.
GURJIT: OK, I'll explain it to her. I'll try to explain it. Look, if – if four is an even number and a hundred is an even number and answers in the four times table are always even – you understand now?
MEHNAZ: Yes, I do know they're even.

In this discussion these children are applying the ground rules of Exploratory Talk. They check with each other before completing the activity on screen by dragging the numbers to the correct boxes. For example, Gurjit asks the other two to explain 'Why do you think that?' and the others explain their reasoning using terms like 'because', 'then' and 'so'. In the final part of the transcript Gurjit undertakes a peer tutoring role, explaining to Mehnaz his general rule, though she rightly seems a little unconvinced by his incomplete reasoning.

Steve Higgins, maths expert and a member of the Thinking Together team, argues that learning maths is like learning a foreign language. He comments that when children are talking about maths to sort and classify numbers it is possible to see their confidence grow because of the support that they receive from the group. Mehnaz, for instance, a girl whose parents come from Bangladesh, begins this exercise apparently very wary of expressing her opinions. She is encouraged to contribute by the others and becomes more involved. The ground rules for talk demand that children must think about and then articulate their understanding of the relationships between numbers. It is this process that enables children to develop their thinking. As Steve Higgins puts it: 'As they talk together using the ground rules they become more fluent speakers of the language of numbers and their relationships which is a central part of the language of maths' (Higgins, 2003).

Shapes

The Israeli maths educator, Anna Sfard, gives a nice example of the difference between novice language and expert language. She uses transcripts of a teacher working with a pair of primary age children who refuse to accept that a long thin pointed shape that the teacher gives them is a triangle (Sfard, 2001). The children are happy that an equilateral triangle is actually a triangle. The problem is that they say the long thin shape looks just like a stick and everyone knows that triangles cannot be sticks. The teacher keeps repeating that if it has three sides and three angles then it is a triangle. Eventually the children agree that it is a triangle but the doubtful way that they say this implies that they do not really believe it.

The problem here is that, in everyday language, the shape on the right of Figure 7.2, shape B, could be called triangular whereas the shape on the left, shape A, would not. It may be called a needle or a stick or a shard but not a triangle, except in the context of mathematics of course. However, as Anna Sfard says, the language of maths is based on a kind virtual reality that children need to be drawn into. In mathematics the appearance of a shape does not really matter. All that is important are abstracted ideas such as numbers of sides and angles.

It can be difficult for children to inhabit the virtual reality of maths. This is where ICT can help. ICT can bring virtual worlds to life. The idea of a triangle is an ideal that is not found in real life. In real life you might find triangular objects but the sides of these objects have no independent existence. However with a simple drawing software package, the picture editor in Microsoft Word for example, it is possible to manipulate sides and points, and angles and lines as if these abstractions were real. Using the triangle tool in such a drawing package, in combination with an interactive whiteboard, it is possible to create an equilateral triangle with angles that can be touched and dragged. In this way children can examine the endurance of the original triangle shape however much it is squashed

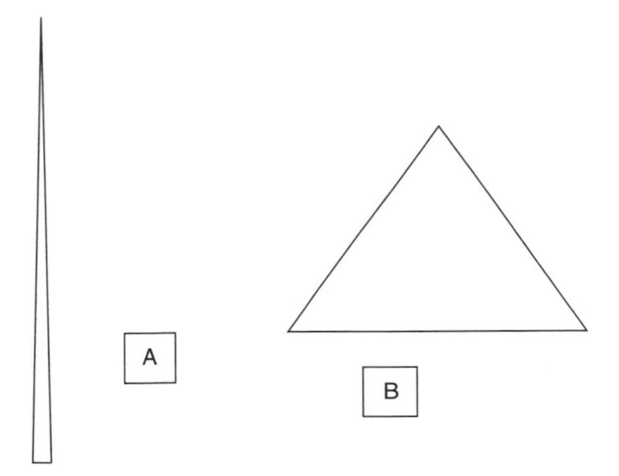

Figure 7.2 Stick versus triangle.

and stretched and made to resemble a stick. The computer, in the very tactile form of an interactive whiteboard, gives a semblance of concrete reality to the abstract idea of a triangle in a way that a teacher's words cannot match. A challenge for group work, after an introductory session with a whiteboard, could be to come up with the most extreme forms possible of familiar shapes and also with shapes that look as if they ought to be familiar triangles or rectangles but actually are not, due to a small deviation.

Problem-solving

Primary maths includes working on logical problem-solving. There are many enjoyable computer games that can help with this area, for example, the Logical Journey of the Zoombinis. This is a critical thinking skills program designed around an escape story. The Zoombinis are a happy group of creatures whose island is taken over by the Bloats. The aim of the game is to help them escape.

Each Zoombini may have one of five kinds of hair styles, eyes or eye wear, nose colours, and feet or footwear. Thus there is the possibility of forming 625 different combinations. Again this game is a way of bringing the virtual reality world of mathematics to life. Zoombinis embody mathematical ideas being similar in their structure to base-5 numbers, and other mathematical objects such as vectors.

In trying to escape the Zoombinis encounter challenges which require deductive logic and creative reasoning. For example, the first obstacle in their path is a pair of rope bridges at the Allergic Cliffs. The guardian of these cliffs sneezes if a Zoombini with the wrong attribute (or combination of attributes) tries to cross the bridge. If too many mistakes are made in attempting this feat, the bridge collapses. This challenge requires children to use sets and evidence to work out how to get all of the Zoombinis across.

At this simplest level, 5- and 6-year olds can complete the puzzles. But the game gets harder the more the players succeed until, at the highest levels of play, the challenges will be difficult for many adults.

Steve Higgins and Nick Packard evaluated the Logical Journey of the Zoombinis with pupils, from age 7 to age 11 (Higgins and Packard, 1999). They found the software to be extremely motivating. It stimulated much useful talk. As part of their evaluation, they noted the following hierarchy of less to more successful problem-solving strategies:

- random attempts with no plan of action;
- randomly trying out a single idea (i.e. forgetting which Zoombinis they had used);
- systematic testing (working through the band of Zoombinis but with no clear hypothesis);
- systematic testing with a single idea;

- suggesting alternatives (some pupils found it difficult to change their minds);
- trying alternatives systematically (but it is easy to lose track!);
- using feedback effectively (i.e. checking their idea was correct both for successful and unsuccessful attempts);
- developing a strategy for a type of problem, attacking it systematically and considering the implications of feedback to reach an effective solution.

Individual work was less effective in generating strategies and often led to extreme frustration when a child did not know how to go on and had no-one to talk to about the problem. Pair and group work were effective. The Thinking Together approach can make pair and group work using games such as Zoombinis even more effective. In addition to the ground rules of Thinking Together, Steve and Nick recommended four specific questions to serve as prompts for partners and groups using this kind of computer activity:

- What is the problem?
- What have you tried?
- What idea are you going to try next?
- How are you going to keep track of what you have done?

Zoombinis and similar games, used as a basis for pair and group work, can help children became more skilful at solving problems and more articulate in explaining their strategies and solutions. The teacher then has the role of drawing out the general principles and explaining how these might apply in other subject areas such as science. The transfer of general problem-solving strategies to other areas can only really occur when the learner has an awareness of the process of their thinking and learning. Children require direct indications of how their thinking in one area can help them by providing a structure useful for another area. It may be crucial that this is discussed and reinforced. For example, the teacher can model the procedure for conducting a fair test to find out which Zoombinis can cross a bridge by testing one attribute change at a time and recording the result. The next step is to make explicit the idea that this same strategy could be used in, for example, testing materials for electrical conductivity in science. In the science lesson it is necessary to remind the children of their prior experience with the Zoombinis before eliciting from them ideas for how to conduct a fair test.

Conclusion

Of all the curriculum subjects, maths perhaps has the greatest potential to appear completely divorced from everyday experience of reality. Here ICT can play an important role in bringing maths to life and giving it concrete form. Even something as simple as the triangle tool in a drawing package can give apparent reality to abstractions. Children playing with the shape of a triangle in a drawing program can directly experience the unity behind the diversity of shapes called 'triangle'. This concrete manipulation gives them a reference for the abstract idea of a triangle.

Seymour Papert made the same sort of argument for the role of computers in learning maths. He claimed that software like LOGO could teach children how to operate in the virtual reality of maths. Computers, he wrote, can transform the abstract ideas of maths into worlds that can be manipulated and therefore directly experienced by children (Papert, 1981). In this way he believed that learning maths, which so often seems an arduous task, could be achieved through painless games.

While agreeing with much of Papert's argument there may be other factors to take into account. Children are social beings and are motivated to learn through their relationships with others, such as parents, teachers and peers. Maths is not only a way of thinking inside an individual mind; it is also a kind of language. That is, maths can offer a form of social communication between people. To become fluent in that language, as with any language, children need guidance and opportunities to practice. Teachers can model ways of talking and can generate contexts in which vocabulary is employed to ensure precise explanations. Children working in groups can offer one another chances to explore their conceptions, to employ their new vocabulary, and an audience for explanation, planning, suggestion and decision making. In this way children learn to speak the language of maths. Challenges and explanations in groups, guided by teachers, can lead children to learn more expert ways of talking.

A combination of a focus on spoken language, both the key words and the specialist ways of questioning, reasoning and problem-solving appropriate to maths, with the support of software can give concrete form to mathematical reality. This combination of talk and computers is a powerful way of helping children to develop their thinking. In this way the Nuffield Thinking Together project demonstrated raised achievement in mathematics.

Summary

The combination of a talk focus and computer-based activities can significantly raise achievement in maths. Developing understanding in maths involves children in learning a new language. To do this they need many opportunities to practice and to be questioned and challenged. Computer software can bring mathematical rules to life. Through manipulating virtual worlds children are helped to understand the artificial reality of maths. Their talk with the teacher and with each other is crucial to the development of understanding. Focused dialogue can contribute to understanding, so that maths activities can become a source of general problem-solving strategies that can be applied across the curriculum and throughout life.

8

ICT AND LITERACY

Using computers to support literacy involves learners in the practical use of spoken and written language. Contact with others generates motivation and provides an audience, with ICT offering flexible tools for rapid, clear communication. Combining ICT use and productive discussion helps the development of the complex skills and understanding that constitute literacy.

T'rrific Tales

When we attended an illustrated talk entitled 'The Classroom of the Future' by Bridget Cooper of Leeds University, we expected to see pictures of somewhere very high-tech and a little austere. In fact the classroom that Bridget and her colleagues had created was as cosy and welcoming as any Key Stage 1 classroom we had encountered. This was perhaps an effect of the warm colours of cushions in the carpet area, the cheerful displays of children's work and the way that the tables were arranged in octagonals for children to work around. Bridget's focus on technology was tempered by a recognition of the importance of emotional experience in learning. Young children, she insisted, need to feel secure and valued if they are to be able to take risks and be creative (Cooper and Brna, 2002). The question that she and her colleagues had set themselves when they received an offer of funding to create 'The Classroom of the Future', was how best to integrate technology into an empathetic teaching approach. This led her to focus on using technology to support learning through dialogues: dialogues between the teacher and the children and amongst the children as well as dialogues with the computer. Her interest in learning through empathy also led her to concentrate on story writing. This was because of an interest in research findings which indicate that story-telling is the most fundamental way in which we convert our feelings into understanding (Damasio, 1999).

At the octagonal tables four pairs of 5- and 6-year-old children were each working with a tablet PC. These look a little like a high-tech version of the slates children used in Victorian days. Although tablets can be used with a keyboard and a mouse, their main feature is an interactive screen which allows children to write on them with a pen (a WACOM PL400). These particular tablets had two pens, as well as a mouse and a keyboard, so that the children could genuinely collaborate on their stories. One child might, for example, start writing the main text while another worked on a picture or filled in the speech bubble of a cartoon character. These small interactive tablets integrated well with a larger interactive screen used for whole class sessions. This allowed teacher-led introduction followed by examples drawn from the children's stories during group work, and whole class plenary sessions to discuss what had been achieved, and how.

The software specially developed for this project, called 'T'rrific Tales' was designed to examine the relationship between software use and the development of literacy. T'rrific Tales combines a number of key features thought to help children create and write stories. Like Bubble Dialogue software it allows children to create cartoon characters and their thought bubbles and speech bubbles. Like the Talking Bug software it has an 'agent' who can help the children but of course this agent, called Louisa, was much more empathetic than our Bug! She was programmed to appear to look at the screen and take an interest in the story, saying things like 'Wow – a witch and a wizard – great!' In addition Louisa helps children with prompts to extend their work, such as 'What sort of a witch is she? – if you want some words to describe her click on "words" under her picture'. T'rrific Tales (see Figure 8.1) has other features that can be found in a range of commercial software such as offering story ideas and frameworks for narratives, making it easy to include pictures, providing relevant and accessible word banks to make typing text less laborious, and speech synthesis to help less fluent writers.

According to Bridget Cooper the children loved the T'rrific Tales software and wanted to work on it all the time. Many in the class said it was their favourite software which is quite an accolade as these children were familiar with a range of commercial games software. The research showed that it helped make their writing more creative and richer in that a range of perspectives were often considered. The stories that the children produced collaboratively on their interactive tablets were very different from those produced using pencil and paper. By the end of the first year of primary school, 5- and 6-year-old children tend to write stories that, while they can be quite lengthy, may have a simple '...and then and then and then...' structure. In addition new writers struggle with presentation, grammar and spelling. The T'rrific Tales stories were shorter and more cartoon-like with lots of pictures and perfect spelling. They were short partly because the children, working in pairs, took full advantage of the opportunity to revise their stories as often as they liked. This concentration on revision might have reduced the quantity of the output but it contributed to its quality and it provided a stimulus and context for productive discussion and reflection.

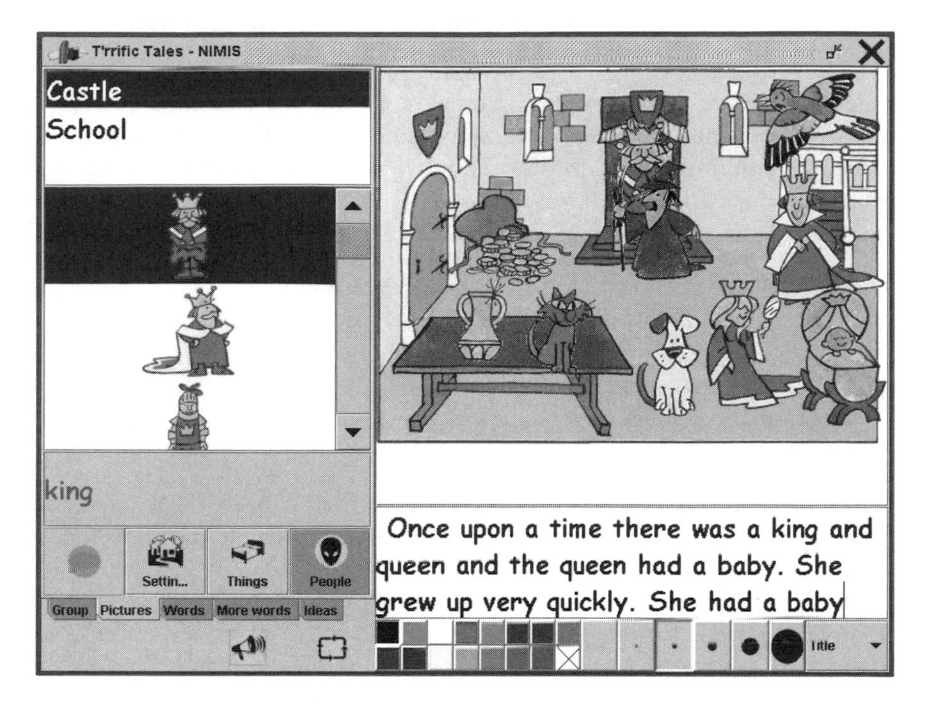

Figure 8.1 T'rrific Tales screen.

T'rrific Tales is not yet available for use in schools. However, its success was based upon features which you can find in many other software packages, such as those listed here:

- Direct, constant guidance and support for writing;
- Provisionality so that changes can be swiftly accomplished and reviewed;
- Word banks so that typed input is minimised;
- Facility to create related graphics;
- Activities for which successful completion depends on dialogue between groups of children and between children and computer.

Some of these are features of standard word processors such as Microsoft Word. One of the key features of word-processing software that can support the development of literacy is the ease with which text can be revised. Young children can be very discouraged by the untidiness of their writing. Software such as T'rrific Tales offers children the motivating possibilities of easy revision and neat finished text.

Literacy and the integration of ICT into classrooms

To be literate is to be able to read and write. However, literacy is often used as a metaphor for other sorts of competence, for example, 'emotional literacy' (able to understand and express feelings) and 'media literacy' (adept with a range of communication media). The use of ICT has generated a further range of literacy adjectives:

- ICT literacy – adept at using (or programming) computers;
- Network literacy – can access, create and interpret web-based documents;
- Multimedia literacy – can move fluently between text, graphics and sound;
- Digital literacy – understands how to use digital information;
- Electronic literacy – understands how to use electronic media to create and interpret texts.

Such modified forms of literacy depend on at least a basic level of classic literacy competence, the language resources for which are developed through speaking and listening.

Literacy is simply the ability to read and write, but reading and writing can take different forms. This ability has historically provided access to power and influence for groups of people and even whole countries. Universal access to books affected the relationship between literacy and power. More recently universal access to computers is also generating change. With Internet technology it is possible to create documents which can be very rapidly accessed by millions of people, with the potential to influence every one of them. The capacity to do so is a sort of power. How this is used and to what purpose depends on people's interests and aims.

For teachers it seems important to acquaint young children with all aspects of technology in settings where uses and purposes can be discussed and considered responsibly. Children have access to computers at home and indeed many children are brilliantly self-taught in terms of skills and knowledge. What talk-focused classrooms offer is the chance to discuss the meaning, for example, of what is found on the Internet and what can be created to share with others. This is a crucial aspect of ICT literacy, almost entirely dependent on the child's capacity to collaborate with others through Exploratory Talk.

In the context of good practice in the use of ICT in education, it is useful to consider literacy as a social practice, that is, to examine how children employ their emerging literacy skills to do things in real contexts. For children in primary schools, developing the capacity to interact effectively with computers requires the teaching of both classic literacy and ICT literacy. These strands of literacy are separable in terms of organising teaching and learning, although it is not necessary to think of literacy as divisible in this way. It's just interesting and instructive to look at, for example, the different ways language is used in print-based media and in the highly graphic and hyperlinked documents of the Internet. A slightly different set of skills and understanding is needed to create and use such different media to best effect. But actually there may be more similarities than differences between them.

For teachers, the problem of what to teach and how to teach it is difficult enough when considering classic literacy. Should we concentrate on a phonic approach, or reading for meaning, or should we employ a mix of methods? What about different learning styles? What are children's literacy needs in school, and should these be promoted over what they require to live the rest of their lives? Should we assess what children can do alone in artificial settings, or in contexts in which their learning really can be applied and put to good use? The teaching and learning of ICT literacy raises all the same questions, and more. Perhaps the way forward is to do what teachers usually do when considering what is really required of education: to gain an understanding of the child's current thinking, and help them to apply their aptitudes and interests to their own development.

Classic literacy, ICT literacy and oracy are interlinked. Ways of writing begin as ways of talking. The transition from reliance on oral language to fluency with written forms does not mean that oracy becomes less important as the child develops. Built on the close relationship between speaking, listening, reading, writing and technical skills, the child's learning in literacy can be thought of as spiralling around lived experience. In this organic conception of literacy, the way that children think is constantly informed by conversations with others, by their experiences and personal reflections and by what they read and write.

Computers, literacy and thinking

The relationship between literacy and thinking seems to be that literacy involves engagement in a constant internalisation of dialogue, whether written or spoken. It also involves generating the individual contributions which create and shape social thinking. The crucial importance of literacy is that it allows us to reflect on the words and phrases we use. In this way, we can become more reflective and analytic users of language (Olson, 1996). Also, higher order thinking such as analysis, synthesis and evaluation happen not just in individual thought but during dialogues. The use of computers with their unique capacity to stimulate, frame and support dialogues in written and spoken form is thus an invaluable asset to classrooms.

For children learning to become literate in school, a distinctive contribution of computers is to offer learners three key things:

1. opportunities to create and modify text with ease;
2. motivating and well-resourced opportunities to engage in learning dialogues with interested others; and
3. opportunities to read and write with an intense level of support from software.

The third of these may seem rather surprising, but writing with specialised software is analogous to learning to talk in the way that most of us do, by using language aloud with others. Computer software can allow children to capture their ideas in written words much more readily than they can if writing by hand. Their text is then available for discussion, reflection and evaluation, that is the sort of creative synthesis, analysis and evaluation which involves higher order thinking.

Evolving language

The ways people use words alters as they hear them used in different contexts by different people, and as people employ words creatively in new combinations to express their thoughts. Word meanings change. Understanding and employing this shifting vocabulary, and contributing to change, is an aspect of becoming literate. The increased use of ICT has created new words (downloads, login) and extended meanings for existing words (menu, button, surfing). In addition hybrid forms which mix the structures of oral and written language have developed in response to the contexts offered by new technologies. For example, Sequence 8.1, 'Party 2nite!', is an example of an online conversation between two 11-year-old school friends. Such literate exchanges are characterised by a lack of conventional grammar and spelling and a mutual understanding of other conventions, developed in order to increase the rate of interaction almost to the speed of talk.

Sequence 8.1 Party 2nite!

STAR SAYS: hellooooo hun!
PUNK ROCK PRINCESS SAYS: Hi! Howz u?
PUNK ROCK PRINCESS SAYS: It was wel funny with ma m8z last night!
STAR SAYS: lol!
STAR SAYS: im fine thanx! ☺ n u?
PUNK ROCK PRINCESS SAYS: Yea! Gr8. A bit tired... lol 2
PUNK ROCK PRINCESS SAYS: N e wayz...wot did u do last night then?
STAR SAYS: nuffin much...still, ive got a party 2nite!

In this sequence 'm8z' = mates and 'lol' = lots of laughs. Punctuation and spelling are erratic and turns may not always be sequential. However, such exchanges have a rationale, syntax and grammar which can be identified by looking at a larger body of similar text. Online dialogue constitutes a new literacy practice, a new variation of language best learned, like any other, by immersion in its community of use. The example has many of the lexical features favoured by 'cool' youth culture. Indeed such features are all the more apparent for being recorded in text rather than vanishing as ephemeral talk.

Star and Punk Rock Princess are drawing on their understanding of the culture in which they live, other cultural models which they emulate, their developing classic and ICT literacy and their own creativity to generate this exchange. It may be of interest to note that both children are high achievers who willingly put their burgeoning literacy skills to use in writing stories, diaries and poems both in and out of school.

In Sequence 8.2, 'txting', similar conventions operate. These are examples of text messages sent by 10-year-old children using mobile phones. Abbreviations are used to speed things up; in this example, they also have the function of reducing the number of characters typed – and so saving money.

Sequence 8.2 txting

- Hey Loz howz u im txting to see r u comin 2day or not? Plz rply cos ive g2g soon! Ella xx.
- Hither:-P lssn I won & u sed I nvr wld didnu? ps c u ltr sk8a.

These abbreviations and syntax have rapidly become so conventional that books of them are on sale in high street shops. In the first message the sender asks for a reply so that she can plan her day. In the second, the sender 'sticks out her tongue' but ends by suggesting an arrangement to meet. These are examples of children putting their literacy to use for their own purposes. They are communicative conversations, uses of written texts to convey meaning. Their form depends on the medium in which they were created, and on the wider context of the community in which the writers operate.

Writing together

Children usually learn to talk before they learn to write. As mentioned earlier, such learning is very often well supported by others who prompt and question and even help to complete words or phrases. The transition from oracy to literacy can be difficult partly because such a support is lacking. The use of computers for writing can help learners by offering support similar to that which we experience as speakers.

An example from the Thinking Together Key Stage 1 project involves a class of 6- and 7-year olds using a reading book called *William and the Guinea Pig* (Rose, 2002). In the story, William is given a guinea pig for his birthday. His little sister Kelly wants to help him look after it but he refuses to let her, saying that she is too young. However, as time goes on William forgets about the guinea pig and begins to neglect it. Kelly looks after it without telling him. This saves the guinea pig and when William's mother goes to look at the animal, all is well. A crisis has been averted. In the last scene in the book, William apologises to his sister and thanks her for her help.

Using pages scanned in to Bubble Dialogue, children were able to voice the thoughts and feelings of the characters at different points of the story. First of all they used audio-tape to record their group's suggestions of what a character might say and what they might be thinking. This created a dialogue to play back, discuss and change. The next step was to produce a written dialogue.

The children found the process of discussion and audio recording straightforward and motivating. Taking on the voices of Kelly, William and their mother in the story helped them to see the story from different points or view and to gain insight into the characters. For example, one group had Kelly repeatedly complaining to her mother that William would not let her help with the guinea pig. The children decided that the mother would patiently explain each time that William had to decide who looked after the guinea pig because he owned it. Meanwhile, in a much more exasperated tone of voice, their mother was thinking: 'Oh give it a rest can't you – you're giving me a headache –.'

After the initial audio recording session the children were asked to listen to their stories and created a written text, often very different from the audio version. The children worked together to generate ideas of what to say and what to write. They also discussed how to write, especially how to spell and use punctuation.

On the whole the children enjoyed the task and were proud of the texts that they produced and were able to print out. The computer-based activity engaged them in the task of writing, breaking the task down into manageable steps and motivating them to produce more focused and thoughtful writing than usual. Used collaboratively, word-processing software can scaffold writing tasks. With the help of other children and the computer learning how to write can become more like learning how to talk. ICT combined with group work can therefore help children over some of the barriers to literacy. Research into the original version of Bubble Dialogue and its support for literacy highlighted increased motivation (Angeli and Cunningham, 1998). Teachers were amazed by the quality and quantity of writing produced by all students including those weak in literacy.

Conferencing

Computers can provide links which help learners move from spoken dialogues to written texts. Writing together can take place through dialogues via computer-mediated communication (CMC), which might be either electronic conferences or exchanges of email. As part of the research described in Chapters 6 and 7, groups in classes from two separate schools were asked to work together using the Oracle conferencing software *think.com*. This provides an online environment through which children can share ideas and contribute text, data or documents for discussion. Schools are provided with email and conferencing links which comply with standards for Internet safety set by the UK government's Department for Education and Skills.

In Sequence 8.3, 'First contact and reply', the children were talking with their group in class and using web-based CMC software to communicate with a group in a different school. This is quite a complex situation. CMC produces a kind of dialogue that is rather different from face to face dialogue. CMC usually generates a sequence of turns, each of which involves an extended and developed 'utterance' or turn in the dialogue. This contrasts with the more rapid, fragmentary and interrupted nature of most face-to-face talk (Wertsch, 2002).

Sequence 8.3 First contact and reply

First contact
HELLO! ... We are class 5M which has fifteen children in it, eight boys and seven girls. We are excited about sending you a message and we will love reading your replies. We are hoping that we will be able to help each other with our Science subject after the Easter holidays... Today in our talking lesson we have a group of three people being videoed. We don't know how they are getting on at the moment but we hope they have remembered all the talking lesson rules....

Reply
Hello there, we have received your message. Thank you for your short note...In our science lessons we are talking about materials. What are you talking about in science? We have mainly been talking about solids/liquids/gases.

The groups' face to face and online discussions were related to a specific collaborative writing task: the creation of a web site about topics in the Year 5 science curriculum. The children were aware that as well as engaging one another in Exploratory Talk, they could apply similar rules to their CMC dialogue in order to generate exploratory writing. In this guided computer-based activity both classes were involved in reviewing their understanding of the science topic, their written communications online, their experience of using the software, and their performance as a 'talk group'. This realised the potential of computers for teaching and learning.

In Sequence 8.4, 'Working well', the teacher intervenes in the work of a group of children engaged in the joint, computer-based writing activity described here. In this example, a group of Year 5 children are revising a paragraph of their email message which they are about to send to their partner group. Its content is the science topic 'How to have a healthy body'.

Sequence 8.4 Working well

TEACHER: Right. Somebody is going to read this to me now.

DECLAN: 'Dear Springdale. In Science we are looking at the healthy human body. We need a lot of exercise to keep our muscles, hearts and lungs working.'

SAMIA: 'Working well.'

DECLAN: 'Working well. It also keeps our bones strong.'

SAMIA: Yes. We don't need a full stop.

TEACHER: Yes. That's fine. That's all right. Carry on. 'Flies..'

DECLAN: 'Flies and other animals can spread diseases and germs. That is why it is very important to keep food stored in clean cupboards, et cetera.'

EVA: Is cupboards spelled wrong? (It is written 'cubourds')

TEACHER: Yes, it is spelled wrong actually. It is cup-boards.

SAMIA: (writing as teacher speaks) b- o- a- r- d- s.

TEACHER: It's a difficult word: c- u- p cup, and then you've got the o- u- makes an 'ow' sound. But it's o- a- , boards.

EVA: o- a- .

TEACHER: OK. Can I ask you a question? – And et cetera is etc, not ect – I want to ask you a question before you carry on. So, why have you felt it is important as a group to send Springdale this information?
(Several children speak together.)

TEACHER: Just a minute. Let's have one answer at a time.

SAMIA: Cause if they haven't done it yet. We can give them the information.

TEACHER: [Yes Samia: .. [that we have found in the book and so when they do get – when they do this part they will know, they will know, so, to answer it.

TEACHER: OK. Excellent. So what were you going to say Declan?

DECLAN: So they can have a healthy body and they can use it for information.

TEACHER: OK.

EVA: And plus, if they haven't got the books.

TEACHER: And if they haven't got the books. Now before you tell me anything else you've found in a book, I think, don't know what you think, do you think it would be a good idea to tell them why you are// what you've just explained to me? We are sending you this information because...

SAMIA: Just because, we couldn't find, something like//

DECLAN: They could be doing it right now.

TEACHER: Well, they might be.

SAMIA: We are sending you this piece of information just in case you haven't done it yet, to help you.

TEACHER: Right, discuss it how you want to say that. OK?

In this interaction, the teacher responds to the children's initial requests for help by providing the correct spelling of 'cupboards' and 'et cetera'. She then introduces a topic which is relevant, in a very different way, to the development of children's literacy. She asks the children to clarify their ideas about the purpose of sending information to the other school. During the ensuing conversation she reminds them to take turns when giving their opinions, and encourages them to achieve an agreement before completing the message. In these ways, she is scaffolding the development of the children's literacy practices. By orientating their attention to the purpose of their written communication she helps the children transcend prosaic features of the task such as correct spelling. Through intervention the teacher directs and models collective thinking with the group. She helps the children to express their ideas orally before writing. (See the box entitled 'Message to Springdale School' for the final text.) In this example, we see a teacher helping the children to achieve success in this collaborative writing task in a way that may help them to work independently in later sessions. The advice we would offer teachers based on this and many similar experiences is to teach Exploratory Talk and ensure that its use is a prominent feature of the ICT-based tasks.

Message to Springdale School

Dear Springdale
In science we are looking at the Healthy Human Body. We need a lot of exercise to keep our muscles, hearts and lungs working well. It also keeps our bones strong. Flies and other animals can spread diseases and germs. That is why it is very important to keep foods stored in clean cupboards, etc. We are sending this information to you just in case you haven't done it yet. We got this information from a book called Children's First Book of Human Body on page 44. If you have not got this book you may find it in a library close to you.

From Declan, Samia, Eva.

More writing together

A wide range of commercial software is available to scaffold the production of stories by allowing children to choose words, frameworks and chunks of text in the same way as T'rrific Tales. The key feature which ICT provides is what might be termed the permanent provisionality of text. This is something so intrinsic to the way ICT works that it is available on standard word-processing software. Other features also support literacy very effectively when put to good use by teachers. One research study of 10- and 11-year-old (Year 6) children asked them to talk and think together in pairs about the choices offered to them by the spelling and grammar checker in Word 97. The findings suggested that, used collaboratively to support reflection in this way, ICT not only enhanced literacy skills but also raised awareness of the structure and variation of language (Lockwood, 2001).

Conclusion

Each individual child faces the challenge of acquiring functional literacy. In school classrooms it is crucial that children are encouraged to engage with a range of literate practices. Some of these forms may not be amenable to conventional assessment but nevertheless are important as part of the rich repertoire of society's practice.

Children's literacy is built on their oracy. Developing speaking and listening skills using ICT-based activities is an effective way to support children through the initial stages of becoming competent readers and writers.

ICT use can enable children's thinking through dialogue with others at a distance as well as nearby. Higher order thinking is developed by the opportunity to engage in Exploratory Talk and writing, and through this to experience collective thinking. ICT has become an invaluable resource for the teaching and learning of literacy, enabling children to draw on the resources of their community and to make their own contribution.

Summary

The thoughtful choice of software and the establishment of a collaborative learning environment can help children to develop confidence as writers. ICT can support the acquisition of literacy particularly well in classrooms where the interrelationship of literacy, oracy and thinking is acknowledged. Computers can offer the sort of support for young writers that they are used to receiving during their efforts to learn to talk. New technology has generated new language forms; children require opportunities to analyse and understand the range of literate practices they will encounter. Teacher intervention during ICT-based literacy activities can ensure that children focus on the communicative purpose of their work.

9

LEARNING THROUGH DIALOGUE IN THE ICT CURRICULUM

While the rest of the book deals with ICT across the curriculum, this chapter focuses on ICT as a subject area in its own right. Many aspects of ICT as a subject are naturally suited to collaborative learning. This chapter indicates how to use a collaborative approach to specific applications of technology such as conferencing, email exchanges, use of the Internet and robotics.

Note: We suggest that you familiarise yourself with the contents of the DfES pack 'Superhighway Safety': http://safety.ngfl.gov.uk/schools/

Talking in the library

Zoe Andrews went along for an introductory visit to the local Technology College. She was with a group of her 11-year-old pupils who would be starting at the college the following September. Looking around the library, she was impressed by the suite of thirty computer workstations. The students seemed to be in a state of flux. Some were seated at computers, while others were standing around or moving from group to group, leaning over to point to the screen or occasionally swapping places with those seated. Some had drinks cans or a sandwich next to the keyboard. 'Are they waiting for their class to start?' she asked. The librarian smiled. 'No; they're working,' she said.

Conventional libraries are quiet places for individual reading. They offer a unique and pleasant environment for those wishing to concentrate and pursue their own thoughts or those of an author. But where there is ICT access, ways of working have developed which reflect the requirements of those using the new information medium. Learning with ICT resources necessitates a different mix of technical and study skills than does learning with books. For learners whose purposes are to do with finding out about aspects of a topic or study area, time spent learning the intricacies of word-processing programmes, spreadsheets, Internet browsers, email systems and so on may seem excessively time consuming. Learners have found that a better way seems to be to start work on your project and find out the technical things you need to know as you go along. A 'just in time learning' approach seems to occur spontaneously wherever groups of people use computers.

The hyperlinked nature of electronic information can mean that even for the most determined, a search focus is easily lost. It can take a long time to find relevant information when searches provide unlimited links to potentially relevant diversions and interesting glimpses of dozens of other areas. The experiences and ideas of others can help to suggest a way through the maze. The chance to ask questions and listen to comments and ideas can generate a very creative way of working. Sharing suggestions and looking at each other's work helps everyone stay on task. Finally, the idea that eating and drinking can help while working is not new; but allowing this in school libraries is – particularly in proximity to expensive machines. The librarian's rationale was that computers are familiar tools at home where drinks and crisps help youngsters to keep going, and that they expected to work in the same way at school.

But what struck Zoe most was the amount and volume of talk. The librarian explained that the introduction of the computers had altered the nature of the work environment. Students expected and indeed needed to talk to one another about what they were doing. What was happening was that students were learning by interacting with each other as much as with the computers. The nature of computers seems to generate much useful social interaction, channelling it into learning.

The conversations that occur in physical space are mirrored in the virtual spaces of the internet, on bulletin boards, newsgroups and email lists where communities share ideas and information. Such virtual conversations are not as ephemeral as spoken conversations. They can be refined into lists of frequently asked questions (FAQs) which with their answers provide a resource for enquiry and reflection.

Zoe considered this experience. She already encouraged her class to talk together in groups. Now, when appropriate, she encouraged them to move around and share discoveries with other groups. She called this 'establishing a community of inquiry' in the classroom. She found that the class ground rules for talk which provided a basis for small group work also supported constructive interaction amongst the whole class. Without the ground rules she was convinced that interacting in this apparently relaxed way would have led to distraction and chaos, but as it was the whole class worked with a shared purpose. Not everything changed however. She still framed activities with introductions in which learning goals were set and conducted plenary discussions in which she orchestrated contributions. She still refused to allow cans of fizzy drinks and sticky snacks anywhere near the school's expensive new keyboards!

ICT can lead to a collaborative and 'just-in-time' way of working with information. This is reflected in the introduction to ICT given in the

National Curriculum:

> Information and Communications Technology prepares pupils to participate in a rapidly changing world in which work and other activities are increasingly transformed by access to varied and developing technology. Pupils use ICT tools to find, explore, analyse, exchange and present information responsibly, creatively and with discrimination. They learn how to employ ICT to enable rapid access to ideas and experiences from a wide range of people, communities and cultures. Increased capability in the use of ICT promotes initiative and independent learning, with pupils being able to make informed judgements about when and where to use ICT to best effect, and to consider its implications for home and work both now and in the future.

The stress in the National Curriculum is on processes – finding, exploring, analysing and exchanging – and developing skills such as creativity, independence and initiative, but these processes and skills are to be developed within the context of using ICT as a medium for communication providing 'rapid access to ideas and experiences from a wide range of people'.

Learning from conferencing

There are many examples of activities involving collaboration over the Internet, from sharing data on the weather to sharing opinions about global current affairs, or presenting local cultural and geographical information for discussion with others. Sometimes the kinds of conversations that result from linking up schools on different continents are of little educational interest. The banality of some email conversations is summed up in the title of one conference paper on this topic: 'It is raining here, what is the weather like where you are?' An example of a more successful and interesting conferencing project is the Warwick project which used a FirstClass conferencing system to link ten primary schools in the United Kingdom with very different cultures and faiths to talk about religious topics. Andrew Raine (1999), reporting on this project, writes: 'We sought to encourage children to find common points of agreement where possible and to demonstrate a respect for different and conflicting viewpoints'.

However, he does not go on to say how this 'encouraging' was done. A conversation that he reports from the conference, selected presumably for its interest to educationalists, goes as follows:

> [Initiation] 'Hello My name is Shenna. I am 10 years old. I think there is life after we die because ghosts are spirits and they come from us. I think life after death is OK because you can sit on clouds and float but you do miss home.'

> [Response] 'Hello our names are Ayesha and Azreen. We also think that there is life after death but we don't agree with you when you say ghosts are spirits and they come from us.
>
> We think that bad people go to hell and good people go to heaven. Every person shall be asked three questions: Who is your God? What is your religion? They will show us a person and ask who is this person? They have to go across a bridge if it shakes you know you are going to hell and if it doesn't shake you know you will go to heaven.'

This certainly indicates the potential of online conferences to allow children to air their views. However, learning to be tolerant requires more than the mere statement of positions: it requires real engagement with others in extended dialogues. In fact it requires Exploratory Talk with questions and reasoning within a co-operative framework. If the potential of conferencing is to be realised, and if real learning is to result, it is important to consider carefully the way in which children communicate. This involves establishing mutual trust and developing shared ground rules for communication.

Although teaching ground rules for talking together face-to-face is an important preliminary to moving into collaborative learning over the Internet, these rules cannot simply be transferred to the new communication medium. Thinking Together talk lessons begin with sessions to build up trust and to share points of view which do not cover the range of experience needed to talk to others using the Internet. An example of an initial 'trust' type exercise to build up a relationship between two classes anywhere in the world, especially for younger children, is for each class to send 'Class Representatives' or mascots to one another. The purpose of the Class Representative (usually a toy animal) is to help give the two classes a shared focus and theme for their communications. It can be taken on class outings, which can then be described to the partner class. It can be given a 'voice' of its own in email communications. It can go to visit individual homes and say what happened there. It can report on the weather or seasonal festivals. It might even get homesick. It can support effective group talk. At the end of the agreed project time, Class Representatives are sent home. (European SchoolNet web site at http://www.eun.org/)

We used this approach to work with two classes of 9-year-old children using the conferencing software *think.com* while working on a topic about Polar Regions. Pairs of children took a particular aspect of the topic (wildlife, weather, people, places, etc.) and collected factual information using a range of resources. They created an 'Information sheet' and posted this on the conference for others to read, consider and evaluate. In a later development, pairs were matched with children in a different school and the group of four created a story together about life in the arctic.

Both the classes that we linked together via *think.com* had worked with a thinking together approach before. The children were asked to develop a set of shared ground rules for using the conference, and reminded that rules of this kind can be enabling rather than prescriptive. A whole class discussion about how to use the *think.com* conferencing area helped to do this. The children decided that something like the ground rules of Exploratory Talk were useful for computer-mediated dialogues, but that there were some new problems which required new rules. For instance, the amount of time that groups had to wait for a response seemed important, so a shared ground rule about when and how often each partner would log on to the system was required.

Ground rules

In your preparation of classes of children for collaborative conferencing activities it may be useful to raise and discuss such issues as listed here.

How to establish identity. Paradoxically, it may be easier to share work with strangers than with those who know you. Perhaps there is the hope that a new audience will be positive about you or at least give you the benefit of the doubt. But it can be difficult to offer creative work to strangers and ask for feedback. Children can usefully discuss questions such as, how much of who we are should we reveal online? What we look like, our personal strengths and weaknesses, details of our lives? Should we imagine ourselves a different person when online? Children using CMC should have the opportunity to consider the advantages and disadvantages of revealing too much or too little, and make decisions about what they think will ultimately help their learning.

How to talk to strangers. What strangers are acceptable? Why is it a good idea to talk with children who might be strangers in classroom settings but not at home when using the computer alone? What privacy is possible in electronic media? A useful way of thinking of any electronic information is that it is like sending a postcard. Anyone and everyone can read it. What implications does this have for considering appropriate vocabulary? At what stages of creative writing do spelling and grammar become important? Crucially, are the ground rules for Exploratory Talk useful as a structure for talking to others online? Why? If not, how might they be modified?

How and why to share information. If an entire group of people offer their ideas and thoughts, will the group do better than each individual could alone? How does this help individual achievement?

Always check your School and LEA Health and Safety Policies before beginning conference activities. Conferencing has the potential to extend the community of inquiry established in one classroom to other classrooms and other communities. However, the effectiveness of communities of inquiry depends on the shared ground rules for communication that are followed within them.

Using email

Many of the considerations raised by conferencing also apply to the use of email. Email can provide more than an exchange of information. It can provide an opportunity for dialogue. Learning dialogues in school settings require a shared purpose and shared ground rules. The implications of this can be illustrated by a brief email exchange between primary schools in the Netherlands reported by Hans Van der Meij (Van der Meij and Boersma, 2002). As we join them two groups of four children in each school are struggling with the task of designing flying machines. They have one email-based lesson each week in which they read their email from the other group and respond; on alternate weeks they work on constructing their machines. Sequence 9.1, We have a tip for you, is an exchange sent in the second week of the project.

Sequence 9.1 We have a tip for you

Second email from Flying Four
Hi Flying Children
You asked us how we construct our plane, which materials we are going to use and how we will let it fly.
We don't know yet how we will construct it, but we think we'll use kite-wood, plastic {trays} and maybe cloth. How we will let it fly we don't know yet
We apologize for knowing so little....
Friday March 19th we went to the library, where we found dewey numbers 659.2, 640.5, 659.6
maybe you can do something with it....
We have a question yet. Which materials do you have and how will you let it fly?...Will you say something about your plane the next time?

Second email from Flying Children
Hello flying four
These are the answers to your questions.
We use triplex for the plane. We throw it in the air. We are going to stand on the climbing frame and throw it away.
We have a tip for you. You can go to a DIY store and ask for cast-away wood....
Would you please mention some titles of books that you use. Because we don't understand that dewey number at all.

Third email from Flying Four
Hi flying children
Here are the titles and authors of the books you asked for:
book 1: Airlines from the author H. J. Highland.

book 2: Inventors from the authors Struan Reid and Patricia Fara....
Thanks also for your tip to visit a DIY store.

The children found these email exchanges extremely motivating. They read the incoming message and discussed what it meant before constructing a shared response. It is interesting to see how they manage, in just three emails, to negotiate rules of clear communication at a distance in order to share useful ideas on how to construct their aeroplanes. At their best, email exchanges can encourage such productive dialogue. Many of the broader aims of the ICT curriculum can be met in successful email exchanges including helping children to develop as independent and creative learners able to use the Internet to learn from and with others.

It can be useful to discuss with children their ideas of what rules apply for communication using email, for example to consider the following questions:

What rules shall we use when sending and receiving email?

- Are there any rules for email in use at home?
- What might go wrong if we don't agree to some rules?
- What should happen if people break our rules?
- What should our rules be?

Teachers can guide classes to establish rules which include an indication that the children understand these important points:

- Language use in email should be appropriate for a general audience. Email should be available to be read by the entire class and by teachers. Email is not a private medium – the lack of privacy can be thought of as similar to sending a postcard;
- Names or pen names must be included on each email sent, and the email should be addressed to a specific recipient in the partner class;
- There may be restrictions on the times when emails can be written or sent: these should be explicit. For example, some schools may expect email to be written off line, while for others this will not be important. Email may be checked at random times, or at set times and it is useful to decide on such practical points in advance;
- Responsibility for who will check mail boxes should be established;
- It is necessary to decide whether email should be stored electronically, and where, or if email is printed, where copies should go;
- There should be sanctions if the rules are broken. Children should be aware that the rules and sanctions are in place to protect and support themselves and people in partner schools.

Advantages and disadvantages of email communication

It is important to help learners to develop an awareness of what can be expected of email communication, and an understanding of its purposes, advantages and limitations. Again this can be a topic for class discussion, during which children contribute their knowledge and understanding of email use at home and in the workplace. You might, for example, organise a discussion along these lines:

Whole class discussion: how and why do we use email?

- Have you used email? Where? For what purpose? What did you think of it as a way of communicating?
- Who has their own email account?
- How was this set up? (i.e. did the child set it up themselves or was it provided by a family member or friend)
- Where and why do other family members use email?
- What are the advantages of email use?
- What are disadvantages?
- What did people do before there was email?
- Do you think most people now communicate by email?
- What difference can communicating by email make to people?
- What sort of things can't you communicate using email?
- Why do you think people who have only talked by email arrange to meet face to face?
- How do you think email might help with school work?

Effective searching on the web

The worldwide web in March 2004 contained about 1,500,000,000,000 pages, that is over a million million pages. It is growing exponentially. Teachers have the responsibility of helping children to understand the nature of the information contained in web pages, how it is produced and why, and to gain an understanding of the benefits and pitfalls of using web-based information. In this way learners become autonomous and can make sensible decisions about the type and quality of information they access.

Problems for children using the web reported by teachers include the following:

- information may be inaccurate or inappropriate;
- the initial aim of a search of the web can easily be forgotten due to distracting links; children sometimes lack a sense of what is relevant;
- left to themselves, even with clear guidance, children frequently conduct searches related to their leisure interests;

- unproductive searches are time consuming and frustrating;
- children may confuse the finding and printing of information from the web with acquiring knowledge or developing an understanding of the topic.

A Thinking Together approach to the use of the Internet offers a solution to some of these problems. The Internet gives access to so much information and so many alternatives that children can be simply overwhelmed. Working and reasoning together as a group can provide the support needed. An effective search of the Internet is essentially a reasoning exercise in which the searcher or group is faced with choices and asked to make decisions as to the best way to go on the available evidence. The distracted, unfocused and poorly prioritised searches which teachers report are often a product of the difficulties children encounter when asked to work alone or as a group who do not know how to talk together.

An associated problem is that teachers may have been encouraged to see their role in working with computers as different from, and less directive than, their usual teaching. The role of the teacher when ICT is integrated into classrooms is often described as that of 'facilitator'. However, in a talk-focused classroom children who are given explicit guidance as to what is expected of them will have access to both information and ways to make meaning from it. Using computers in groups, children *can* be left to learn for themselves – but with peer support, sensitive teacher intervention and the structure of the ground rules to enable joint construction of meaning. The crucial task for the teacher is to integrate computer-based talk activities with the larger ongoing conversations of the classroom. By this process, children working at the computer are still held within the ties and motivating force of a relationship with the teacher and with the class.

Information can be found in books or on the web; but in themselves texts and web pages do not *know* anything. Knowledge only exists when someone reads a book or web page and understands what is being said. Children seek to understand things for socially defined purposes as part of ongoing dialogues and relationships. What they find on the Internet must be brought into dialogues and integrated into the larger dialogue which is the construction of shared understanding in the classroom.

A three-part structure to lessons, that is whole class work followed by small group work using computers and then back to whole class work, is an effective framework for the integration of computers into the curriculum. Within this structure, the teacher can establish issues and aims at the beginning and then return to these in a whole group plenary session at the end to examine what children have learnt, and how, and to check that the lesson aims have been achieved. Through this cyclical process children can become aware that their talk together at the computer, or communication with others through the computer, can make a huge contribution to their learning. It is important that talking and thinking are included in the aims given to the class for each activity so that the class knows that discussing issues, ideas and decisions is not an optional extra but a crucial part of what they are meant to be doing.

A key question which children can ask one another when engaged in Internet searches is, 'How does this information help with our shared purpose?' A useful activity for developing discrimination is to take a selection of web sites offering information about the same topic and ask the children which they trust most and why. Exploratory Talk provides a tool to raise critical awareness of the quality of information on the web.

Interactive whiteboards

Thoughtfully used, whiteboards can be a terrific focus for collaborative work. The large screen allows tasks and information to be readily shared and discussed. The most useful functions of interactive whiteboards seem to be to do with enabling overlay, annotation and effective sharing of children's work and ideas. Collaborative activities for whole classes and groups can involve joint problem solving with a shared end product. For example, the National Numeracy Strategy site suggests interactive activities for classes such as use of the board to present pupils' work or as a 'digital flipchart'. The whiteboard can allow children to collaborate with one another in the same way as they might while working in a small group, with opportunities for invaluable teacher intervention. Ultimately, it is the teacher's selection of software, the structuring of the activity within the context of the lesson, and the guidance of pupils towards clearly understood learning objectives which ensure that whiteboards are put to good use in classrooms.

Robotics

Robotics in the form of programmable Roamers are part of primary ICT curriculum. The 'Robofesta-UK' (Johnson *et al.*, 2002) association organise events where groups of children build robots together, often in competition with other groups. But robot-kits are expensive. A recent activity of Robofesta, in conjunction with the BBC, illustrates a less expensive way of bringing robots into the classroom. In 2002 the BBC children's programme Blue Peter issued a challenge to children to design robots. Winners had the chance to travel to Japan, the home of Robofesta International, to build their robots. But even without building any robots many children exercised their creativity while having fun with this competition. Over 32,000 designs were submitted.

The children were challenged to design a *really useful robot*. The Robofesta UK team, based at the Open University, wanted children to be creative and to focus their energies on something constructive. The team

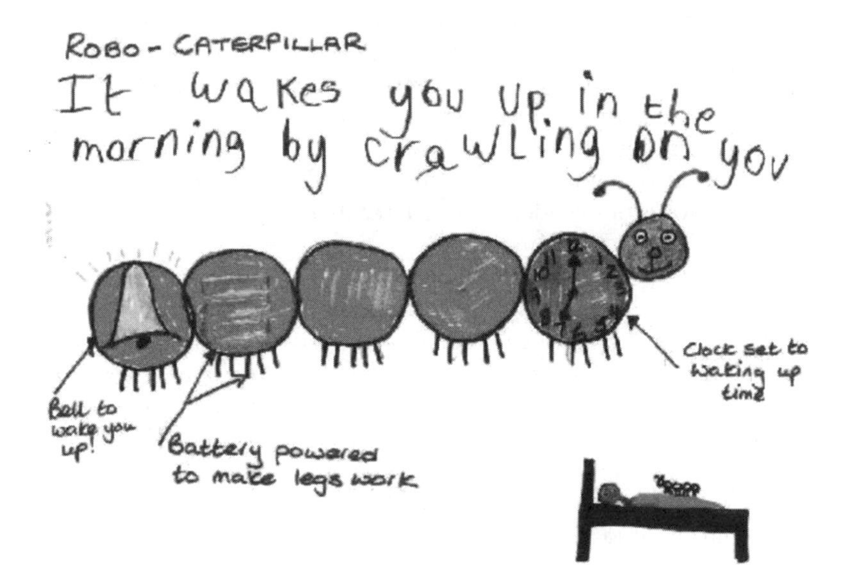

Figure 9.1 The RoboCaterpillar to wake you up by crawling on you! (First Prize, 'seven and under'. Designer: Steven Sutton, aged 6.)

wanted to build on the interest in the *robot wars* genre of television programmes but in contrast widen it by encouraging children to think about robots which could make a positive contribution to human life.

The children were instructed to say what their robot does (specification) and how it does it (analysis). They were also encouraged to come up with designs 'that could really work' (evaluation). This reflected the educational aim of helping the children to understand better the nature of design. Although children entered this competition individually the design activity involved naturally lent itself to collaboration and Exploratory Talk.

The first prize in the 'seven and under' group went to Steven Sutton for his splendidly imaginative robot to wake you up in the morning (Figure 9.1).

Establishing a community of practice

Tim Denning (University of Keele) met with a group of teachers to determine some guidelines for good practice in teaching and learning with ICT. His report which is available on the Becta web site (http://vtc.ngfl.gov.uk/uploads/application/CharacteristicsofGoodPractice-44745.pdf) makes for valuable reading. One thing the teachers agreed was essential was what Tim described as: 'A safe environment for failure, to encourage genuine trial, honest evaluation and improvement based on experience and constructive collaboration.'

This describes the community of inquiry atmosphere that the Thinking Together approach can help to establish in classrooms. Another interesting recommendation from the group is the promotion of critical self-assessment of activities and outcomes. Again this fits into the Thinking Together practice of always asking groups to evaluate how they worked together, what problems they encountered and how they solved them or could solve them. Tim's group also recommended that ICT teachers collaborate to share good practice.

> Good practice in ICT teaching is evolved and shared most effectively where there are local professional networks. It can be very reassuring to encounter similar problems shared by colleagues, and to have the chance to look at examples of authentic tasks and other creative ideas.

ICT teachers suggested the following strategies with the aim of ensuring the continual sharing of ideas and expertise:

- Regular meetings with like-minded colleagues to pool resources and note common issues.
- Opportunities to talk to others, including the chance to become involved in debating ideas and defending them.
- Communication networks, conventional or electronic, encompassing schools and staff from a wide area.
- Meeting with colleagues and discussing best practice. Finding ideas of new ways to deliver topics.

This suggests that a collaborative approach is as good for teachers as it is for learners. The medium of ICT makes collaboration more possible. Open University courses in the use of ICT for example have produced a community of 50,000 teachers linked through a FirstClass conferencing system in which they are able to exchange information about classroom practice and learn from and with each other.

Conclusions

The ICT curriculum is naturally rich in opportunities for collaboration, both within and beyond the classroom. This is probably related to the way that groups seem to gather spontaneously around any new technology trying to understand it and make it work. Teachers can harness such social learning opportunities to help children learning within the curriculum. Without guidance group work can be too demanding and children can easily become distracted. Computers can support the establishment of a community of inquiry amongst groups of teachers and learners.

Summary

Educational ways of working with computers continue to evolve as teachers and learners generate highly social uses of ICT. But nothing is ever all good, and some serious problems can arise where children are using computers to communicate. A classroom atmosphere of openness can alert young people to potential pitfalls, while discussion of the issues involved can raise awareness of good practice.

Dialogue between children using Internet resources can help them to generate knowledge and understanding from the information they find. Specific technologies such as roamers and interactive whiteboards are now part of the teacher's toolkit, employed in conjunction with learning objectives to facilitate curriculum learning. In such circumstances, whole class and individual benefit can be gained through discussion. The chance to listen to children as they articulate their thoughts provides teachers with opportunities to assess learning and intervene when and where necessary. For teachers, sharing both problems and solutions can help everyone to continue to provide creative and engaging lessons in which the tools of ICT are integral.

10

CONCLUSION

Raising achievement

This chapter brings together the main themes of the book. We summarise the Thinking Together approach to ICT across the curriculum and indicate how this can raise achievement in primary classrooms.

Measurable learning outcomes in curriculum subjects are important in schools, but it is also important to improve children's capacity to think and to learn. Chapter 3 describes how higher order thinking skills of individual children originate in dialogues through which they learn to reason, to evaluate, to create new understandings together and to provide relevant information. It is now widely accepted that children can learn how to think and learn how to learn through being drawn into dialogues in which they are questioned, challenged and extended (Hobson, 2002). Learning dialogues are characterised by a shared search for understanding and a willingness to listen and to change. In learning dialogues different perspectives are brought together to help all participants to develop their ideas. Through engaging in such dialogues with others, both teachers and peers, children can be motivated by the desire to understand and to be understood.

There is a convergence between this social and 'dialogic' view of learning and the specific potential of ICT within education. Chapters 5–9 describe how ICT-based activities can effectively support and resource peer learning dialogues in a range of ways in different curriculum areas. Through the organising work of teachers, the tools ICT offers can be employed to resource and support the long-term learning dialogues of a classroom community. It is this focused use of ICT to support learning dialogues within the curriculum that can raise children's achievement. That is, children can not only increase their test scores but also develop their capacity to engage effectively in thinking and learning dialogues with others and, indeed, with themselves.

Working with teachers to promote the use of Exploratory Talk in classrooms, the Thinking Together research team did not anticipate an impact on the government's standard measures of literacy and numeracy – the Key Stage 2 national assessment commonly referred to as SATs. One evening (July, 1998) the Education Secretary at that time, David Blunkett, appeared in the national television news naming schools whose pupils had made substantial gains as measured by SATs results. The name of one of the three 'most improved' schools that he mentioned was familiar; it was one of the Thinking Together primary schools. Teachers at the school confirmed that the children who had done so well in the SATs were the same classes which had been using the Thinking Together approach throughout the previous year. There were certainly other factors at work in their achievement, but the teachers were convinced that the improvement in SATs results was strongly related to the children's improved speaking, listening and thinking skills (Lovelock and Dawes, 2001).

The causal link between the increased use of Exploratory Talk and improvements in SATs results may not be immediately obvious. The children had worked to improve the educational quality of their dialogues in small groups whereas SATs are taken individually in settings which do not allow talk. As we explained in Chapter 3, following the ground rules for Exploratory Talk improved the ability of children to solve reasoning test problems when they were working together; the puzzle is why this should also improve the performance of those same children when working alone. The explanation seemed to be that some individuals who had not initially performed well on reasoning tests had improved their performance by internalising the kind of learning dialogues that they had practised with their group.

This idea was investigated by asking individual children who were familiar with the Thinking Together approach to talk aloud as they solved reasoning test problems. Despite working alone they 'talked to themselves' as if still in a discussion group. They asked themselves questions such as, 'Why do I think it is that one?'. They gave reasons for their choices and they considered alternatives before making a final decision. Perhaps something similar had happened during their SATs; perhaps they had talked themselves through the problems using an internal dialogue.

After this unexpected result in one school it seemed important to arrange a more careful and convincing test of the impact of the Thinking Together approach on curriculum learning. This became possible through a research project funded by the Nuffield Foundation, as described in Chapters 6 and 7. The findings can be briefly summarised. Using official test questions given at the beginning and again at the end of the year the Thinking Together classes increased their SATs scores significantly more than classes which were similar in every other respect.

However, it is evident that educational achievement cannot always be measured by SATs scores. We intended primarily to enable children's participation in effective learning dialogues. Throughout the book, there are illustrations of children learning together in different curriculum areas such as Science, Maths and Citizenship through dialogues stimulated, resourced and framed by computer software. Through engaging one another in Exploratory Talk, children were seen to construct understanding for themselves. The kind of learning that results has been characterised as 'deep' learning, that is, learning which is assimilated by the learner because it has personal meaning and is organised as part of a coherent whole. This can be contrasted with the kind of 'shallow' learning in which information is memorised, facts and concepts are associated unreflectively, and tasks are directed towards the demands of assessment (Marton and Saljo, 1976). Enabling children to become participants in learning dialogues can promote deep learning in all curriculum subjects. Computers are invaluable resources for this enterprise.

The role of ICT

ICT helps teachers and learners to create interesting classroom environments where interactivity and opportunities to communicate enable all to participate. Computers help teachers to generate authentic tasks which are meaningful for children. In addition computers are motivating machines when activities are set at the right level of challenge. The range and scope of software means that ICT use can enrich all curriculum subjects. Importantly, computers serve as an excellent focus and resource for small group work. With the right combination of teaching and software, computers can stimulate and direct learning dialogues in such a way as to achieve curriculum learning goals.

The I*D*RF educational exchange structure involves computer-initiated discussion with children talking together before making a collective response. The computer then provides feedback or a follow-up to their response. This computer-supported I*D*RF interaction is important because it combines directive teaching and active learning into a single activity. Prompts, information and questions can provide directive teaching while learning dialogues with one another enable children to construct new understandings and generate new questions.

I*D*RF exchanges are one powerful way to use computer-based activities to raise achievement. Computers can also support learning dialogues in a more open-ended way. Bubble Dialogue, for example, along with similar 'open-ended' software, supports dialogue without offering 'feedback' or 'follow-up', except for the rewarding experience of children's own voices bringing to life a cartoon character. Bubble Dialogue and similar software give children the chance to think aloud in a way that encourages joint reflection on what is said. Computers are especially useful here because any text created can be quickly and easily modified in the light of group reflection. A group might, for example, consider what would happen to the outcome of their story if a character responded differently at any point.

Simulations and control technologies can provide helpful ways to engage with a variety of ideas and situations. Chapter 7 describes a simple triangle graphics tool which offers an interactive resource to stimulate discussion and help children understand the properties of the shape. Using this tool, discussion offers everyone the chance to reflect on the information the computer provides, drawing on previous learning and generating new learning. The conversation is then a resource for each individual as they separately amend their conception of 'triangle' to make new meanings and connections.

Papert's 'powerful idea' for children working with computers was that the computer could make abstract mathematical ideas more concrete and therefore more accessible. However, as the evidence presented in Chapter 3 suggests, software on its own is often not enough. Learning does not reliably arise from such interaction. Conversations with focused group mates can give real significance to that experience.

Email and electronic conferencing (or any type of computer-mediated communication or CMC) allows children to express their thoughts and consider what it is they really wish to say. Chapters 8 and 9 describe how CMC allows children to take part in stimulating and purposeful conversations with people at a distance. Chapter 5 discusses the potential of CMC to support citizenship education by enabling children to participate in moral and political debates in wider communities than the classroom. What is interesting about such computer-mediated links is that the rapidity and facility of the communication (in terms, e.g. of things like expense and accessibility) means that *more* communication is possible. This means that there is more chance to share understanding. However, it is actually very difficult to do so; it is impossible to say whether participants in a dialogue ever really share understanding. There are too many subtle and complex aspects within any topic to match all of them with another person. But it is easy to verify if members of a group share a *lack* of understanding! The chance to express ideas, by talking with others using the resources offered by computers, helps children to know their own minds as they identify points of disagreement with others. Challenging others and accepting challenges provides children with new information and ideas, and the chance to change their minds in a supportive context. The value of this as a continuous process, taking place in classrooms where learning goals are explicit and a variety of peer opinion can be drawn on, cannot be overstated.

The role of the teacher

In classroom settings teachers have a crucial role in ensuring that children understand the aims for their work with computers. The way teachers establish learning objectives, convey the nature and purposes of tasks, and create a climate of collaborative enterprise, all make a substantial difference to how well ICT helps children to develop their thinking and learning.

The Thinking Together approach promotes a collaborative or 'dialogic learning' (Alexander, 2002) approach in which children are aware of the importance of their talk together. The success of the approach rests on teachers, who are responsible for the following (amongst a myriad other things):

- The teaching and learning of explicit speaking and listening skills which promote thinking together;
- Organising computer-based activity to support children's learning of speaking and listening skills and their subsequent use of Exploratory Talk for learning in curriculum areas;
- Providing introductory and closing plenary sessions to establish and review learning objectives for speaking and listening in addition to those for curriculum learning;
- Sensitive intervention in group work to model Exploratory Talk and support group discussion.

Chapter 2 indicates how the teacher might prepare children for group work. The teacher's professional knowledge and expertise during intervention ensures that discussion helps children to grasp key concepts. For example in science, Chapter 6 demonstrates how the intervention of the teacher ensures that Exploratory Talk stimulated by software aids learning. The combination of the teacher's introduction and the software focused the talk of the children on planning a fair test, making predictions and offering explanations. The ICT-based activity allowed the children to test their ideas, in this case to check which material makes a good sound insulator. The children's misconception (metal is a better sound insulator than cork) meant that their working hypothesis proved incorrect. The group discussion allowed children to articulate their ideas in a way which allowed the teacher to 'see' their reasoning and help them to consider other factors (density or 'compactness' of material). The cognitive challenge the children faced was that of changing their conception of what made a good insulator. Their difficulty was overcome by the startlingly effective combination of stimulating software, teacher intervention and productive dialogue.

In citizenship the relationship between Exploratory Talk and curriculum learning is different. One of the aims of the curriculum is the reasoned discussion of moral issues. Exploratory Talk about moral dilemmas such as those offered by 'Kate's Choice' directly achieves this aim. Chapter 5 describes the convergence between drawing children into discussion with one another through Exploratory Talk and the kind of moral development that is an aim of the PHSE and Citizenship curriculum. Participation in Exploratory Talk and moral development both require a capacity to listen to others and consider a range of alternative view points.

The kind of questions teachers, or computers, ask in citizenship lessons are often rather different from those in science or maths lessons. In citizenship a typical question might be 'How do you think Kelly felt when William refused to let her look after his guinea pig?' or 'What do you think Mrs Cook would say about children stealing from her shop?' This is not the same kind of question as 'What is your prediction?' or 'How many sides does a triangle have?' However, the same ground rules for Exploratory Talk help groups to support each others learning in order to advance their understanding. The teacher adds value to such questions by emphasis on the adherence to this way of talking and by making the learning purpose of their discussion evident to children. A good discussion is in itself a real achievement, not always easy even for those adults who claim to know how to do such things.

ICT has a unique capacity to support learning dialogues. Teachers can make use of this capacity through first empowering children with the skills that they need to participate effectively in learning dialogues and then through establishing ICT-based contexts for learning from dialogue across the curriculum. Learners are hugely advantaged by a teacher's foresight in planning, structuring and organising activities which employ the powerful tools of ICT and spoken language together to advance learning.

Summary

A Thinking Together approach to computer use can raise achievement in curriculum subjects. If education is considered as developing a capacity to engage effectively in learning dialogues, the use of computers to resource such dialogues is invaluable. Referring to examples in the book, we indicate that a focus on talk helps children to understand better the process of collaborative learning which is a feature of their classroom life. Computers offer teachers and learners powerful ways to use spoken language to think and learn together. The teacher has a crucial role in helping children to understand how and why to talk to one another. Without such teaching, computer-based activities may disappoint. For the individual child, the chance to collaborate with a talk-focused group of classmates may only ever happen when the teacher has so organised it. During these moments, the child is privileged by access to the two most powerful resources people have created – spoken language and new technology.

NOTES

INTRODUCTION

1 You can read more about the Thinking Together approach in Dawes *et al.* (2000) *Thinking Together*, Questions Publishing.

1 USING COMPUTERS IN CLASSROOMS

1 Viking England. Designers: R. Thistleton and J. Dary. Fernleaf Educational Software Limited.

3 THINKING TOGETHER

1 A shorter version of this chapter first appeared in Teaching Thinking. R. Wegerif, 'Group Intelligence', *Teaching Thinking*, 2000, 3(3), 24–27. Birmingham: Questions Publishing.
2 © J. C. Raven Ltd: these are 'parallel' items especially produced for this book.
3 This is an old story much used in PHSE education. A version of it can be found in a collection by Idries Shah, *The Exploits of the Incomparable Mulla Nasrudin*, New York: Octogon Press, 1995.

6 SCIENCE, TALK AND ICT

1 This is a modified version of the Open University's Elicitation Engine software.

BIBLIOGRAPHY

Alexander, R. (2002) *Culture and Pedagogy: International Comparisons in Primary Education*. Oxford: Blackwell.

Angeli, C. and Cunningham, D. J. (1998) 'Bubble Dialogue: tools for supporting literacy and mind', in C. Bonk and K. King (eds) *Electronic Collaboration: Learner-Centred Technologies for Literacy, Apprenticeship and Discourse*. New York: Lawrence Erlbaum Associates, pp. 81–101.

Bakhtin, M. (1986) *Speech Genres and Other Late Essays*. Austin, TX: University of Texas Press.

Bakhtin, M. and Volosinov, V. (1986) *Marxism and the Philosophy of Language*. Cambridge, MA: Harvard University Press.

Buzan, A. and Buzan, B. (2000) *The Mind Map Book*. London: BBC.

Carver, S., Lehrer, R., Connell, T. and Ericksen, J. (1992) 'Learning by hypermedia design: issues of assessment and implementation', *Educational Psychologist*, 27(3), 385–404.

Claxton, G. (1999) *Wise-Up: The Challenge of Lifelong Learning*. London: Bloomsbury.

Cooper, B. and Brna, P. (2002) 'Supporting high quality interaction and motivation in the classroom using ICT: the social and emotional learning and engagement in the NIMIS project', *Education, Communication and Information*, 2(2–3), 113–138.

Crook, C. (1994) *Computers and the Collaborative Experience of Learning*. London: Routledge.

Damasio, A. (1999) *The Feeling of What Happens: Body, Emotion and the Making of Consciousness*. London: Vintage.

Dawes, L., Mercer, N. and Wegerif, R. (2000) *Thinking Together: A Programme of Activities for Developing Thinking Skills at KS2*. Birmingham: Questions Publishing.

De Corte, E. (1990) 'Towards powerful learning environments for the acquisition of problem-solving skills', *European Journal of Psychology of Education*, 5, 5–19.

Denton, T. (2003) Characteristics of good practice. Available online at: <http://vtc.ngfl.gov.uk/uploads/application/CharacteristicsofGoodPractice-44745.pdf> (accessed 25th July 2003).

DfES (2003) The National Curriculum. Available online at: <http://www.nc.uk.net> (accessed 25th July 2003).

Dillon, J. (1988) *Questioning and Teaching: A Manual of Practice*. London: Croom Helm.

Fernandez, M. (2001) 'Collaborative writing of hypermedia documents and the social construction of knowledge', Paper presented at the 9th European Conference for Research on Learning and Instruction: Bridging instruction to learning, Fribourg, Switzerland, August.

Fisher, E. (1992) 'Characteristics of children's talk at the computer and its relationship to the computer software', *Language and Education*, 7,187–215.

Gibbons, P. (2000) 'Learning a new register in a second language', in C. Candlin and N. Mercer (eds) *English Language Teaching in its Social Context: A Reader*. London: Routledge.

Goleman, D. (1996) *Emotional Intelligence*. London: Bloomsbury.

Harris, M. and Butterworth, G. (2002) *Developmental Psychology – A Student's Handbook*. Hove, East Sussex: Psychology Press.

Higgins, S. (2003) 'Parlez-vous mathematics?' in I. Thompson (ed.) *Enhancing Primary Mathematics Teaching*. Buckingham: Open University Press.

Higgins, S. and Packard, N. (1999) 'Teaching logical thinking with the Zoombinis', *Teaching Thinking Magazine*, 1, 12–15.

Higgins, S. and Packard, N. (2002) *Thinking skills and ICT pack*, MAPE.

Hirst, A. and Garner, S. (2003) 'Learning from designing the RoboFesta-Blue Peter Robots', AROB-2002, International Conference on Artificial Life and Robotics, in M. Sugisaka (ed.), Oita University, January 2002. Available online at: <http://robofesta.open.ac.uk/> (accessed March 2004).

Hobson, P. (2002) *The Cradle of Thought: Exploring the Origins of Thinking*. London: Macmillan.

Howe, C., Tolmie, A., Duchak-Tanner, V. and Rattray, C. (2000) 'Hypothesis testing in science: group consensus and the acquisition of conceptual and procedural knowledge', *Learning and Instruction*, 10(4), 361–391.

Hughes, M. (1990) 'Children's computation', in R. Grieve and M. Hughes (eds) *Understanding Children*. Oxford: Basil Blackwell.

Independent ICT in School Commission (1997) *The Stevenson Report*. Available online at: <http://rubble.ultralab.anglia.ac.uk/stevenson/ICTUKIndex.html> (accessed 25th July 2003).

Inkpen, K., Booth, K. S., Klawe, M. and Upitis, R. (1995) 'Playing Together Beats Playing Apart, Especially for Girls'. Proceedings of Computer Supported Collaborative Learning (CSCL) '95. Lawrence Erlbaum Associates, pp. 177–181. Available online at: <http://www.cs.sfu.ca/people/Faculty/inkpen/publications.html> (accessed 25th July 2003).

Johnson, J., Hirst, A. and Garner, S. (2002) 'Learning from designing the RoboFesta-Blue Peter Robots', AROB-7, Proceedings of International Symposium on Artificial Life and Robotics, in M. Sugisaka and H. Tanaka (eds), ISBN4-9900462-2-6, Oita University, January 2002.

Jonassen, D. (2000) *Computers as Mindtools for Schools: Engaging Critical Thinking, 2nd edn*. New Jersey: Prentice Hall.

Jonassen, D., Carr, C. and Yueh, H. (1998) Computers as Mindtools for Engaging Learners in Critical Thinking, *TechTrends*, 43, 24–32.

Kruger, A. (1993) 'Peer collaboration: conflict, cooperation, or both?' *Social Development*, 2(3), 165–185.

Lockwood, M. (2001) 'Checking on the checker – using computers to talk about spelling and grammar', in P. Goodwin (ed.) *The Articulate Classroom: Talking and Learning in the Primary School*. London: David Fulton Publishers.

Loveless, A. (2000) 'Creativity, visual literacy and information and communications technology', in D. M. Watson and T. Downes (eds) *Communications and Networking in Education: Learning in a Networked Society*. Norwell, MA: Kluwer Academic.

Loveless, A. (2002) *Creativity, Technology and Learning: A Review of the Literature for NESTA FutureLab*, 2002. Available online at: <http://www.nestafuturelab.org/papers> (accessed March 2004).

Lovelock, T. and Dawes, L. (2001) 'Thinking Together', *Teaching Thinking*, 2(1), 25–27.

McMahon, H. and O'Neill, W. (1993) 'Computer-mediated zones of engagement in learning', in Tom Duffy, J. Lowyk and D. Jonassen (eds) *Designing Environments for Constructive Learning*. NATO Advanced Studies Institution Series: Springer-Verlag.

Marton, F. and Saljo, R. (1976) 'On qualitative differences in learning I: outcome and process', *British Journal of Educational Psychology*, 46, 4–11.

Mercer, N. (1995) *The Guided Construction of Knowledge*. Clevedon: Multilingual Matters.

Mercer, N. (2000) *Words and Minds: How We Use Language to Think Together*. London: Routledge.

Mercer, N., Wegerif, R. and Dawes, L. (1999) 'Children's talk and the development of reasoning in the classroom', *British Educational Research Journal*, 25, 95–113.

Mercer, N., Wegerif, R., Dawes, L., Sams, C. and Higgins S. (2003) *Language, Thinking and ICT in the Primary Curriculum: Final Project Report to the Nuffield Foundation*. Milton Keynes: Open University, 2002. Available online at: <http://www.thinkingtogether.org.uk> (accessed March 2004).

Monk, R. (1991) *Ludwig Wittgenstein: The Duty of Genius*. Harmondsworth: Penguin Books.

Naylor, B. and Naylor, S. (2000) *The Snowman's Coat and other Science Questions*. London: Hodder Children's Books.

Neisser *et al.* (1996) 'Intelligence: knowns and unknowns', *American Psychologist*, 51(2), 77–101. (This is the report of an American Psychological Association task force on the issue of intelligence.)

Olson, D. (1996) *Modes of Thought: Explorations in Culture and Cognition*. New York: Cambridge University Press.

Papert, S. (1981) *Mindstorms*. Brighton: Harvester.

Papert, S. (1993) *The Children's Machine: Rethinking School in the Age of the Computer*. New York: Basic Books.

Perkins, D. and Salomon, G. (1989) 'Are cognitive skills context bound?', *Educational Researcher*, 18(1), 16–25.

Raiker, A. (2002) 'Spoken language and mathematics', *Cambridge Journal of Education*, 32(1), 45–60.

Raine, A. (1999) *Using Information and Communications Technology in the Teaching of Primary R. E. Farmington Fellows Report 74, The Farmington Trust*. Available online at: <http://www.farmington.ac.uk>.

Raven, J., Raven, J. C. and Court, J. H. (1998) *Raven Manual: Section 1. General Overview*. Oxford Psychologists Press.

Resnick, L. (1987) *Education and Learning to Think*. Washington, DC: National Academy Press.

Rojas-Drummond, S., Velez, M., Gomez, Laura, Mendoza, A. and Perez, V. (2001) 'Exploratory talk as a discursive tool to promote reasoning among elementary school Mexican children', Paper given at 9th Conference of EARLI Fribourg, August.

Rose, G. (2002) *Thinkers: William and the Guinea Pig*. London: A&C Black.

Roth, W. (1994) 'Student views of collaborative concept mapping: an emancipatory research project', *Science Education*, 1, 1–34.

Roth, W. and Roychoudhury, A. (1994) 'Science discourse through collaborative concept mapping: new perspectives for the teacher', *International Journal of Science Education*, 16, 437–455.

Scanlon, D., Deshler, D. D. and Schumaker, J. B. (1996) 'Can a strategy be taught and learned in secondary inclusive classrooms?' *Learning Disabilities Research & Practice*, 11(1), 41–57.

Scardamalia, M. and Bereiter, C. (1991) 'Higher levels of agency for children in knowledge building: a challenge for the design of new knowledge media', *The Journal of the Learning Sciences*, 1(1), 37–68.

Selwyn, N. (1998) 'The effect of using a home computer on students' educational use of IT', *Computers and Education*, 31(2), 211–227.

Selwyn, N. (2002) Citizenship, technology and learning: a review of the literature for NESTA FutureLab, 2002. Available online at: <http://www.nestafuturelab.org/papers> (accessed 25th July 2003).

Sfard, A. (2001) 'There is more to discourse than meets the ears: looking at thinking as communicating to learn about mathematical learning'. Keynote address given at EARLI 2001, Freiburg, Switzerland, 29 August 2001.

Shah, I. (1995) *The Exploits of the Incomparable Mulla Nasrudin*, New York: Octogon Press.

Sinclair, J. and Coulthard, R. (1975) *Towards an Analysis of Discourse*, Oxford: Oxford University Press.

Sterne, J. (2004) *Learning and Teaching RE with ICT*. Buckingham: Open University Press.

Street, B. (1997) 'The implications of the "new literacy studies" for literacy education', *English in Education*, 31(3), 45–59.

Styles, I. (1999) 'The study of intelligence: the interplay between theory and measurement', in M. Anderson (ed.) *The Development of Intelligence*. Hove, East Sussex: Psychology Press.

The NASA education site (2003) Available online at: <http://kids.msfc.nasa.gov/Earth/Moon/> (accessed 25th July 2003).

Van Boxtel, C., Van der Linden, J. and Kanselaar, G. (2000) 'Collaborative learning tasks and the elaboration of conceptual knowledge', *Learning and Instruction*, 10, 311–330.

Van der Meij, H. and Boersma, K. (2002) 'Email use in elementary school: an analysis of exchange patterns and content', *British Journal of Educational Technology*, 33(2), 189–200.

Vygotsky, L. (1986) *Thought and Language*. Cambridge, MA: MIT Press.

Vygotsky, L. (1991) 'The genesis of higher mental functions', in P. Light, S. Sheldon and B. Woodhead (eds), *Learning to Think* (pp. 34–63). London: Routledge.

Wegerif, R. (1996) 'Using computers to help coach exploratory talk across the curriculum', *Computers and Education*, 26, 51–60.

Wegerif, R. (1997) 'Factors affecting the quality of children's talk at computers', in R. Wegerif and P. Scrimshaw (eds) *Computers and Talk in the Primary Classroom*. Clevedon: Multi-lingual Matters, pp. 177–189.

Wegerif, R. (1998) 'The social dimension of asynchronous learning networks', *Journal of Asynchronous Learning Networks*, Vol. 2. Available online at: <http://www.aln.org/alnweb/journal/vol2_issue1/Wegerif.pdf> (accessed 25th July 2003).

Wegerif, R. (2000) 'Group Intelligence', *Teaching Thinking*, 3(3), 24–27 (Birmingham: Questions Publishing).

Wegerif, R. (2002) *Thinking Skills, Technology and Learning: A Review of the Literature for NESTA FutureLab*. Available online at: <http://www.nestafuturelab.org/papers> (accessed 25th July 2003).

Wegerif, R. and Scrimshaw, P. (1997) *Computers and Talk in the Primary Classroom*. Clevedon: Multilingual Matters.

Wegerif, R., Mercer, N. and Dawes, L. (1999) 'From social interaction to individual reasoning: an empirical investigation of a possible socio-cultural model of cognitive development', *Learning and Instruction*, 9, 493–516.

Wells, G. (1999) *Dialogic Inquiry: Toward a Sociocultural practice and Theory of Education*. Cambridge, UK: Cambridge University Press.

Wertsch, J. (2002) 'Computer, Mediation, PBL, and Dialogicality', *Distance Education*, 23(1), 105–108.

Whitebread, D. (1997) 'Developing children's problem-solving: the educational uses of adventure games', in A. McFarlane (ed.) *Information Technology and Authentic Learning*. London: Routledge.

Wittgenstein, L. (1951/2001) *Philosophical Investigations*. London: Blackwells.

Wood, D. (1988) *How Children Think and Learn*. Oxford: Basil Blackwell.

Wood, D., Bruner, J. S. and Ross, G. (1976) 'The role of tutoring in problem solving', *Journal of Psychology and Psychiatry*, 17, 89–100.

INDEX